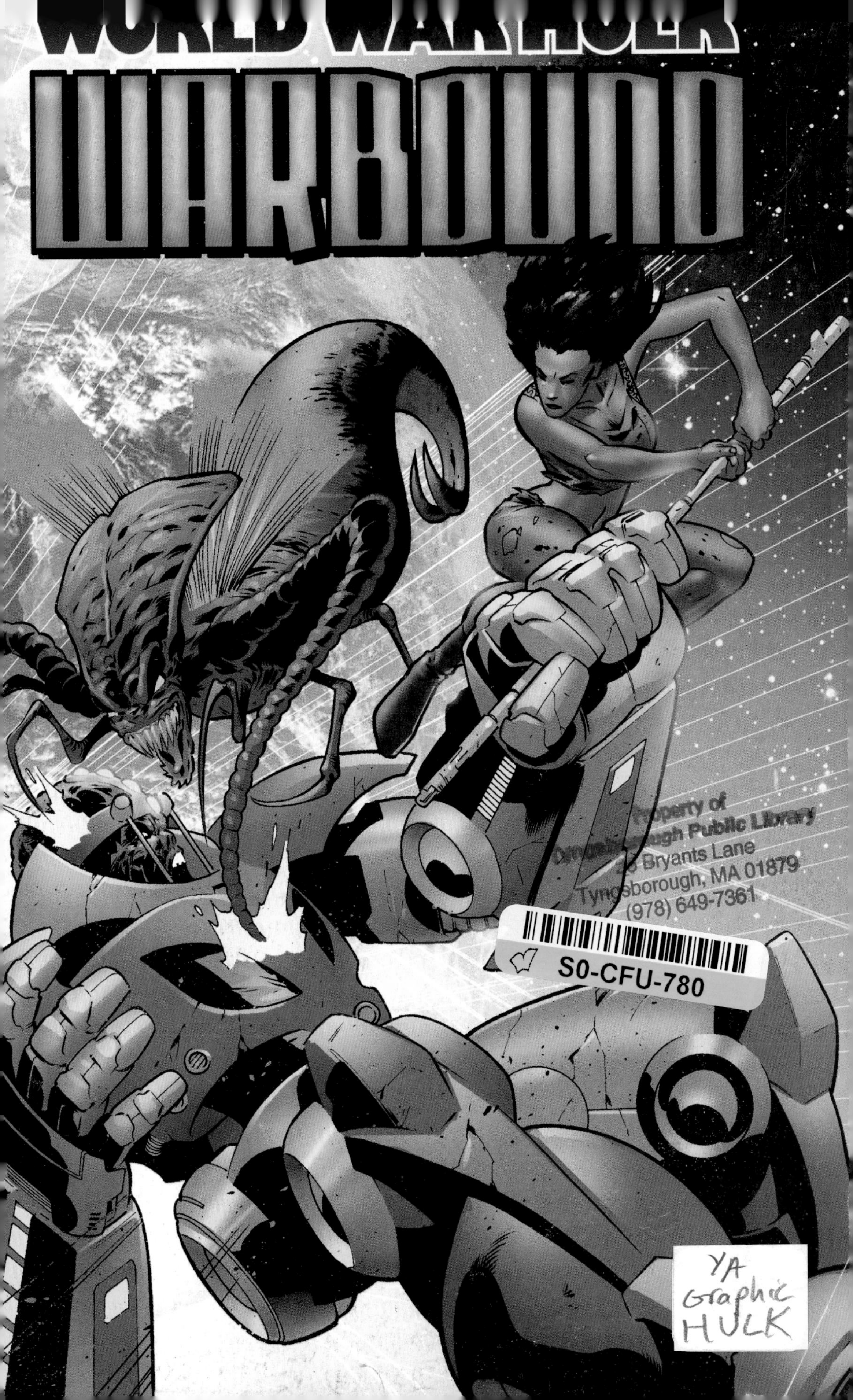
WORLD WAR HULK
WARBOUND

# WORLD WAR HULK
# WARBOUND

Writer: **GREG PAK**
Artist: **LEONARD KIRK** with
**GARY MARTIN** (Inks, Issue #5)
Colorist: **VAL STAPLES**

## "TALES OF THE WARBOUND"
Writer: **GREG PAK**
Penciler: **RAFA SANDOVAL**
Inker: **ROGER BONET**
Colorists: **MARTEGOD GRACIA**
& **MOOSE BAUMANN** (Part Two)

Letterer: **VIRTUAL CALLIGRAPHY'S JOE CARAMAGNA**
Cover Artists: **JIM CHEUNG**, **JOHN DELL**, **JUSTIN PONSOR**
& **JASON KEITH**

Assistant Editor: **NATHAN COSBY**
Editor: **MARK PANICCIA**

Collection Editor: **CORY LEVINE**
Assistant Editor: **JOHN DENNING**
Editors, Special Projects: **JENNIFER GRÜNWALD**
& **MARK D. BEAZLEY**
Senior Editor, Special Projects: **JEFF YOUNGQUIST**
Senior Vice President of Sales: **DAVID GABRIEL**
Book Design: **RODOLFO MURAGUCHI**

Editor in Chief: **JOE QUESADA**
Publisher: **DAN BUCKLEY**

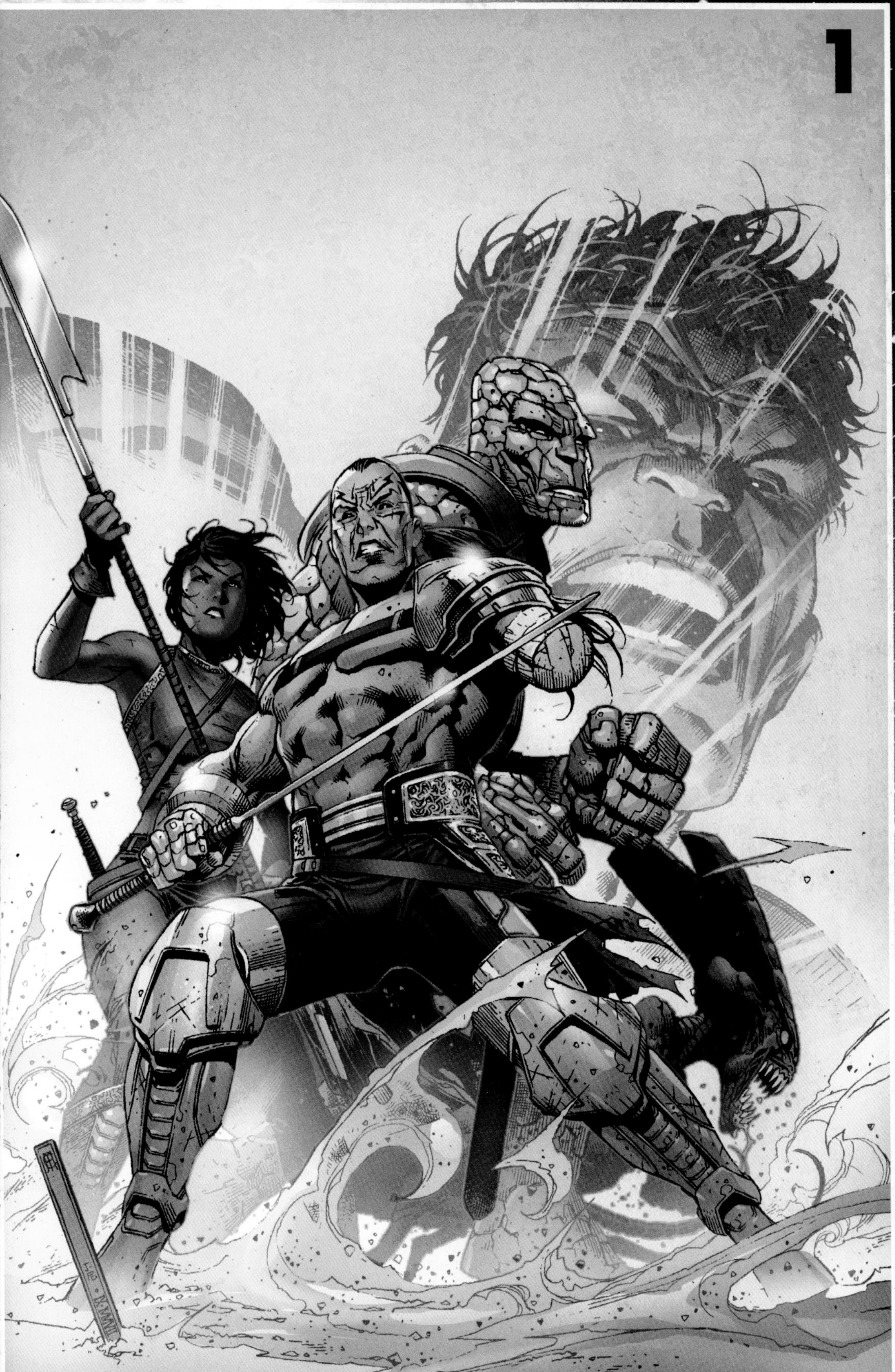
1

# S.H.I.E.L.D. UNIT 42B DAILY DIRECTIVE

MISSION: Apprehend the last four at-large members of the alien army that attacked New York during World War Hulk.

KORG

ELLOE KAIFI

NO-NAME
OF THE BROOD

HIROIM
THE OLDSTRONG

Subjects may be injured and weakened, but have sworn an oath to stand by each other to the death.

Maximum force authorized.

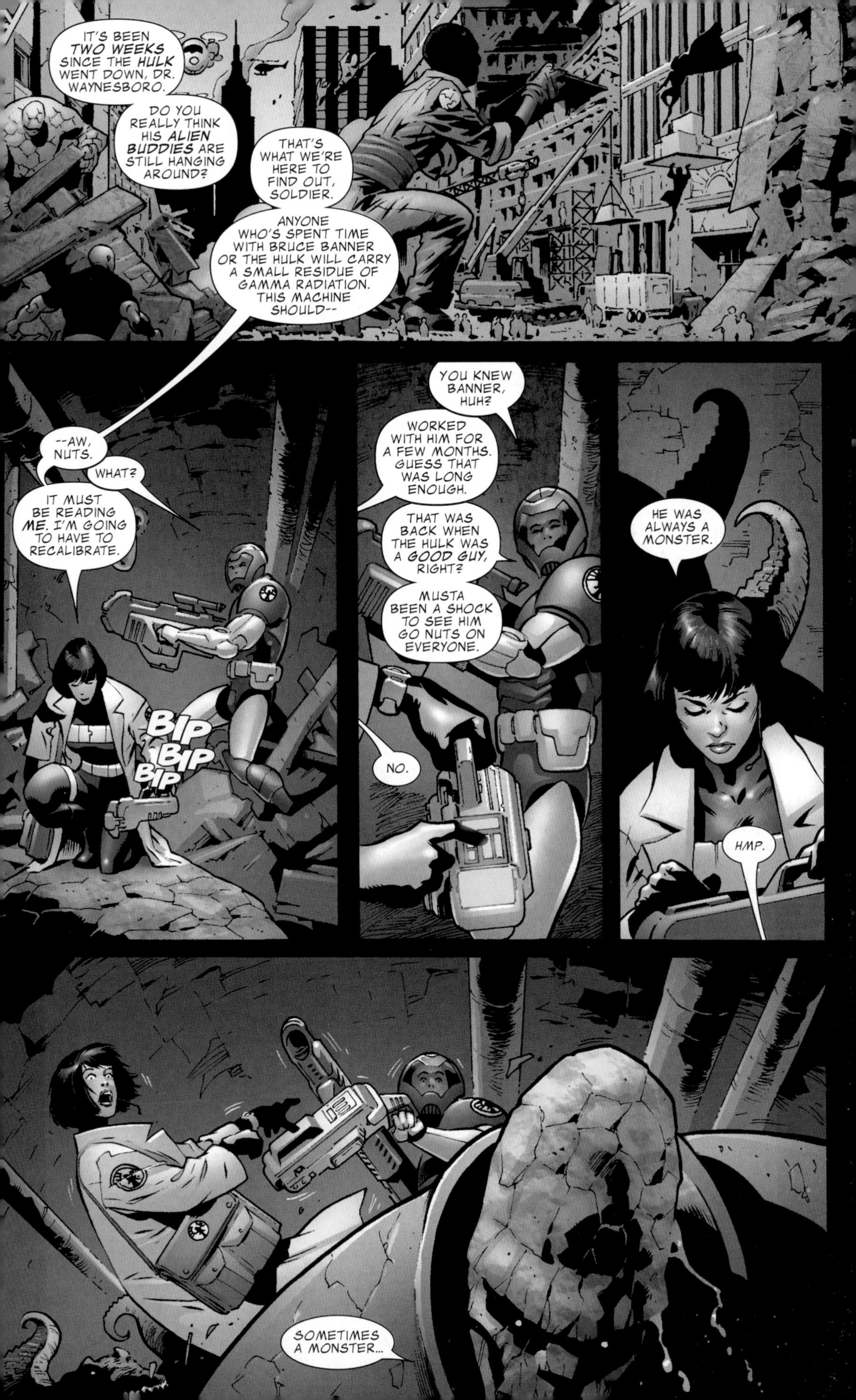
IT'S BEEN TWO WEEKS SINCE THE HULK WENT DOWN, DR. WAYNESBORO.
DO YOU REALLY THINK HIS ALIEN BUDDIES ARE STILL HANGING AROUND?
THAT'S WHAT WE'RE HERE TO FIND OUT, SOLDIER.
ANYONE WHO'S SPENT TIME WITH BRUCE BANNER OR THE HULK WILL CARRY A SMALL RESIDUE OF GAMMA RADIATION. THIS MACHINE SHOULD--
--AW, NUTS.
WHAT?
IT MUST BE READING ME. I'M GOING TO HAVE TO RECALIBRATE.
BIP BIP BIP
YOU KNEW BANNER, HUH?
WORKED WITH HIM FOR A FEW MONTHS. GUESS THAT WAS LONG ENOUGH.
THAT WAS BACK WHEN THE HULK WAS A GOOD GUY, RIGHT?
MUSTA BEEN A SHOCK TO SEE HIM GO NUTS ON EVERYONE.
NO.
HE WAS ALWAYS A MONSTER.
HMP.
SOMETIMES A MONSTER...

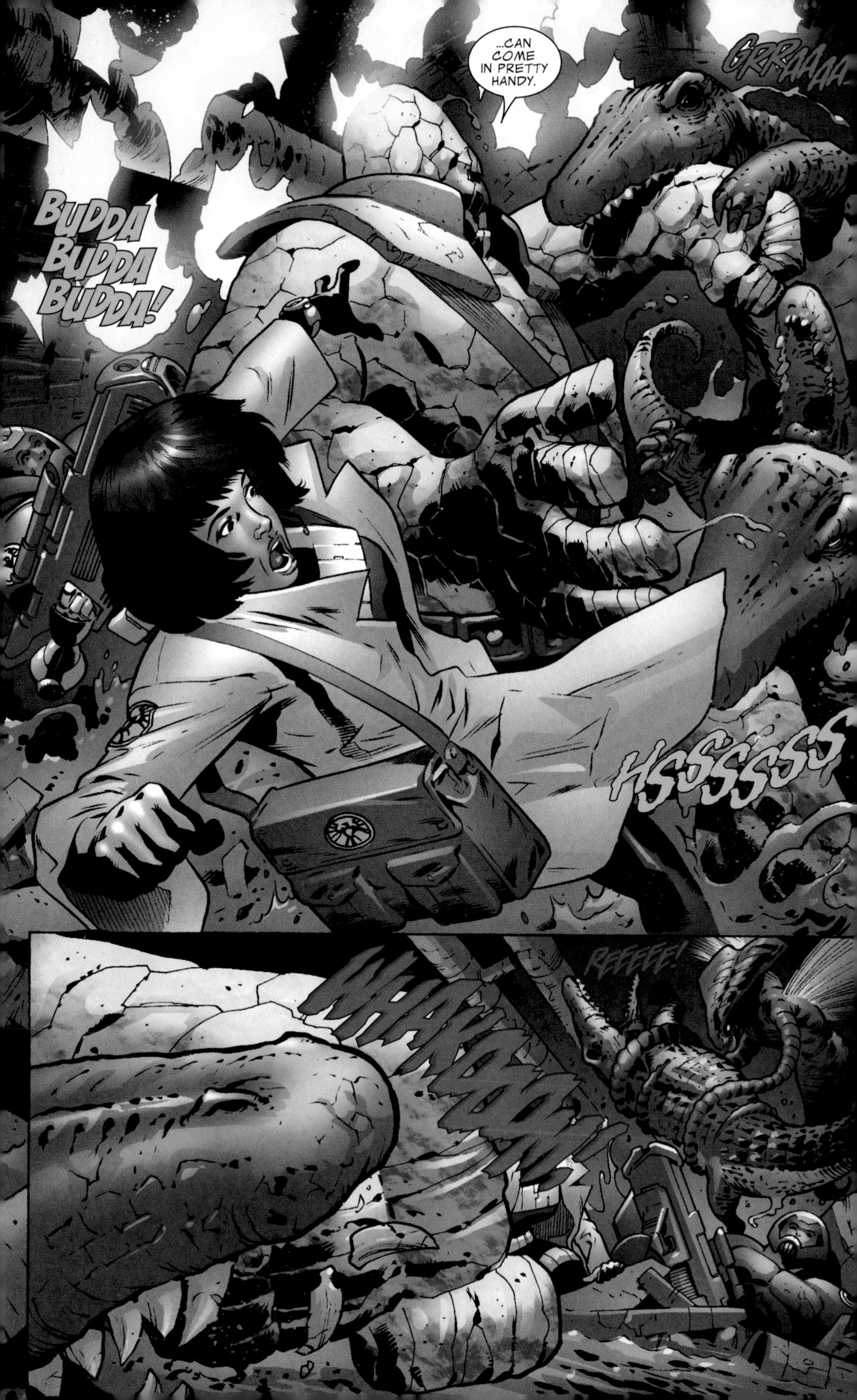
...CAN COME IN PRETTY HANDY.
GRRAAAA
BUDDA BUDDA BUDDA!
HSSSSSSS

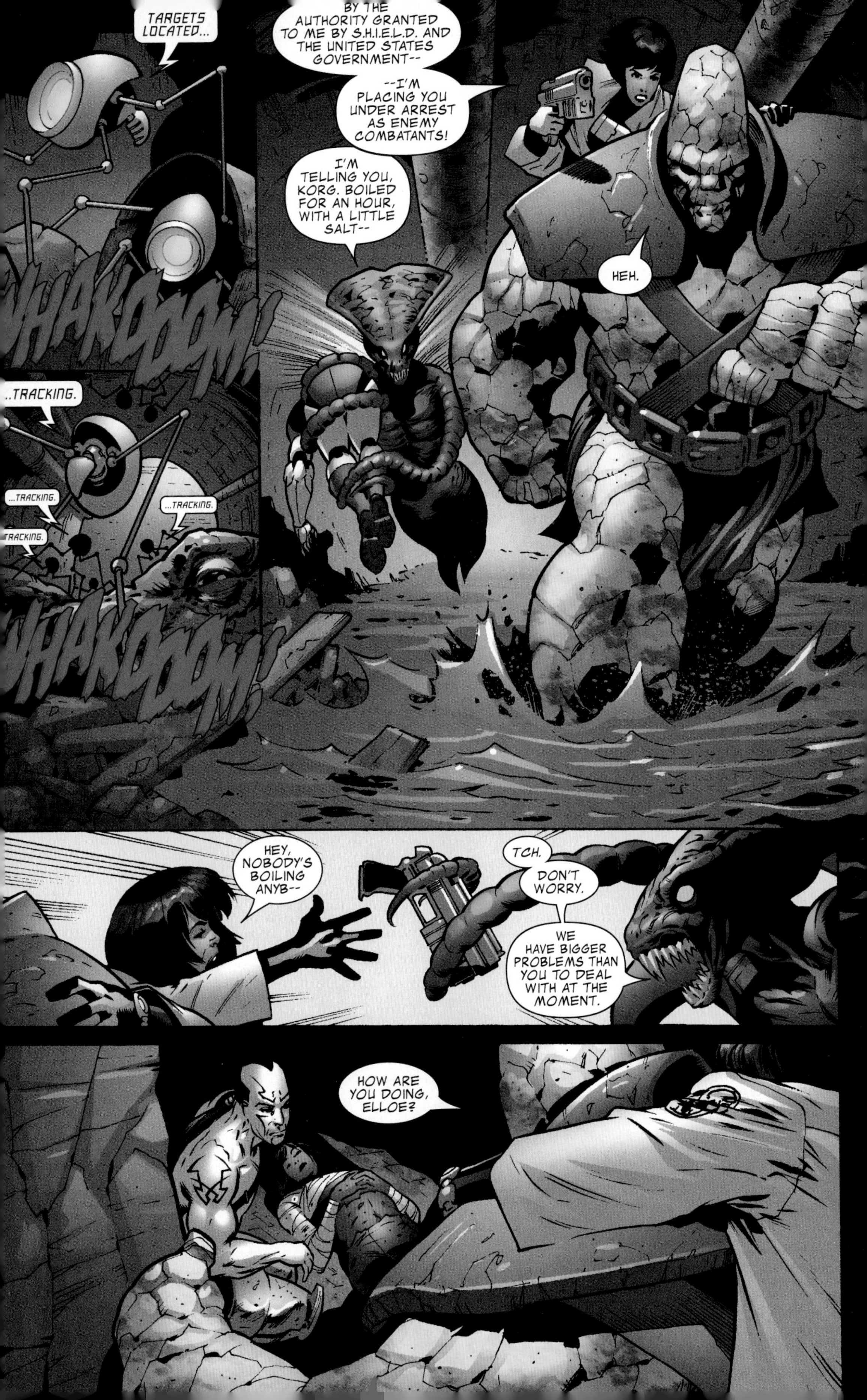
TARGETS LOCATED...
BY THE AUTHORITY GRANTED TO ME BY S.H.I.E.L.D. AND THE UNITED STATES GOVERNMENT--
--I'M PLACING YOU UNDER ARREST AS ENEMY COMBATANTS!
I'M TELLING YOU, KORG. BOILED FOR AN HOUR, WITH A LITTLE SALT--
HEH.
..TRACKING.
...TRACKING.
...TRACKING.
TRACKING.
HEY, NOBODY'S BOILING ANYB--
TCH.
DON'T WORRY.
WE HAVE BIGGER PROBLEMS THAN YOU TO DEAL WITH AT THE MOMENT.
HOW ARE YOU DOING, ELLOE?

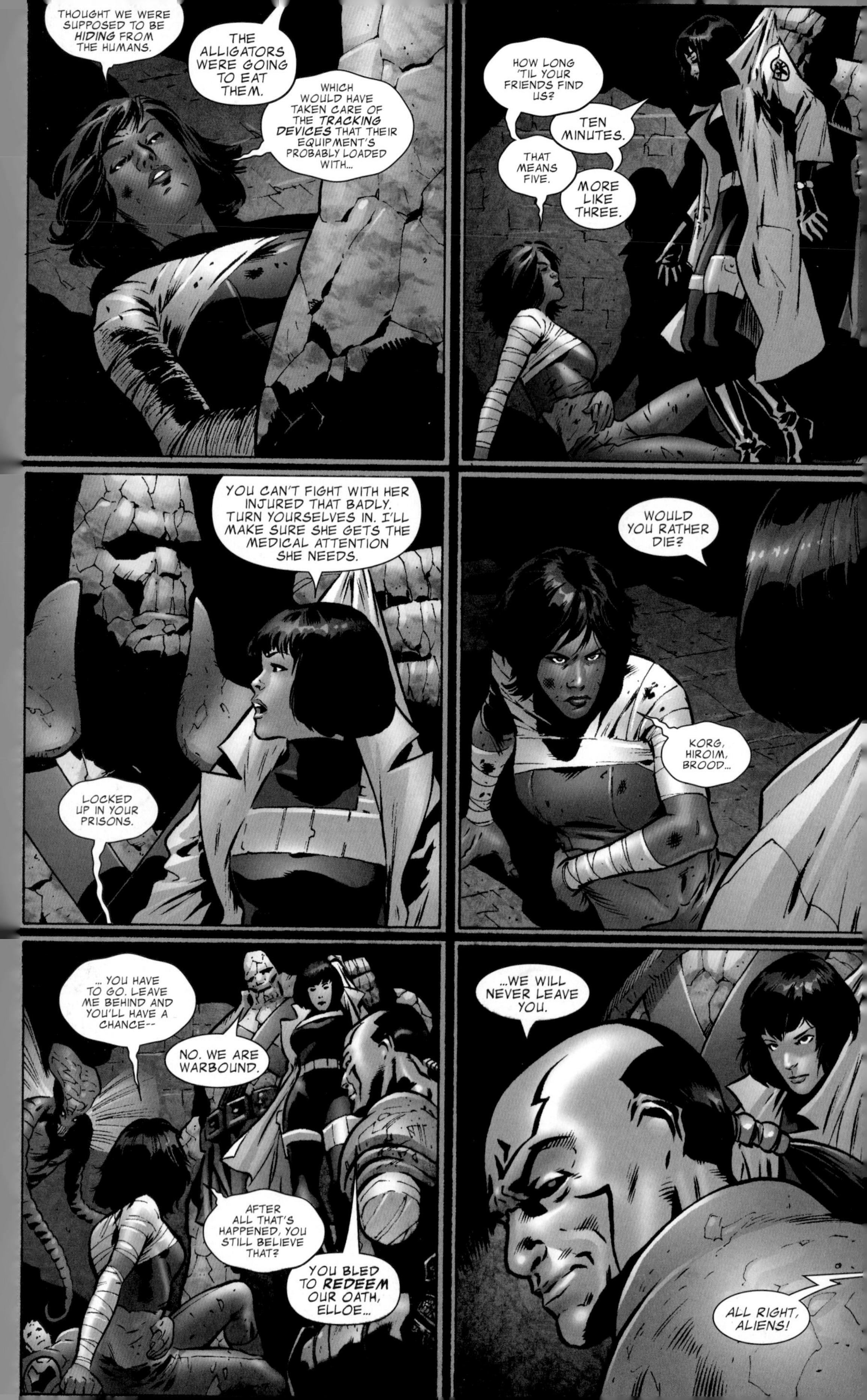
THOUGHT WE WERE SUPPOSED TO BE HIDING FROM THE HUMANS.
THE ALLIGATORS WERE GOING TO EAT THEM.
WHICH WOULD HAVE TAKEN CARE OF THE TRACKING DEVICES THAT THEIR EQUIPMENT'S PROBABLY LOADED WITH...
HOW LONG 'TIL YOUR FRIENDS FIND US?
TEN MINUTES.
THAT MEANS FIVE.
MORE LIKE THREE.
YOU CAN'T FIGHT WITH HER INJURED THAT BADLY. TURN YOURSELVES IN. I'LL MAKE SURE SHE GETS THE MEDICAL ATTENTION SHE NEEDS.
LOCKED UP IN YOUR PRISONS.
WOULD YOU RATHER DIE?
KORG, HIROIM, BROOD...
... YOU HAVE TO GO. LEAVE ME BEHIND AND YOU'LL HAVE A CHANCE--
NO. WE ARE WARBOUND.
AFTER ALL THAT'S HAPPENED, YOU STILL BELIEVE THAT?
YOU BLED TO REDEEM OUR OATH, ELLOE...
...WE WILL NEVER LEAVE YOU.
ALL RIGHT, ALIENS!

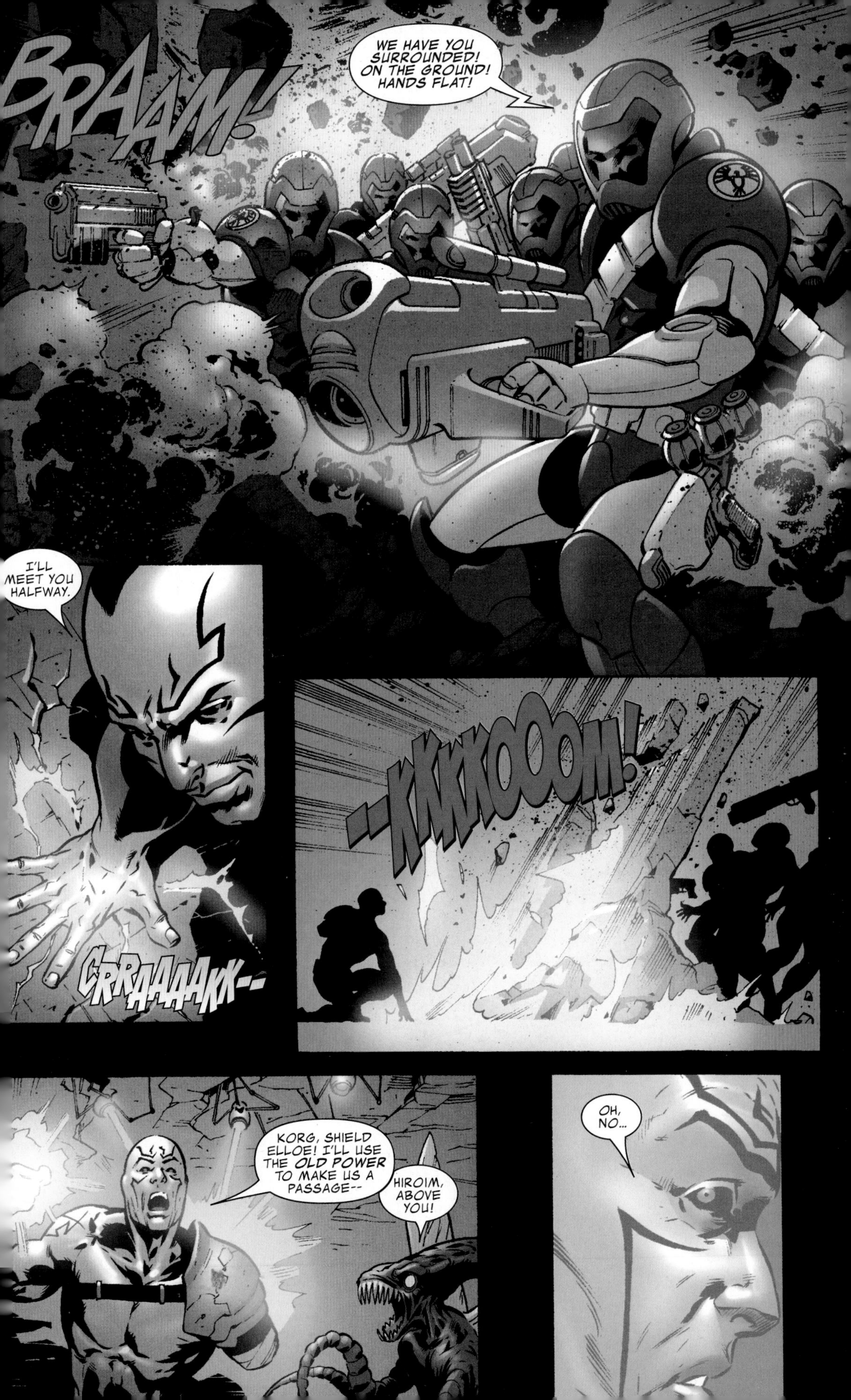

BRAAM!
WE HAVE YOU SURROUNDED! ON THE GROUND! HANDS FLAT!
I'LL MEET YOU HALFWAY.
CRRAAAAKK--
--KKKKOOOM!
KORG, SHIELD ELLOE! I'LL USE THE OLD POWER TO MAKE US A PASSAGE--
HIROIM, ABOVE YOU!
OH, NO...

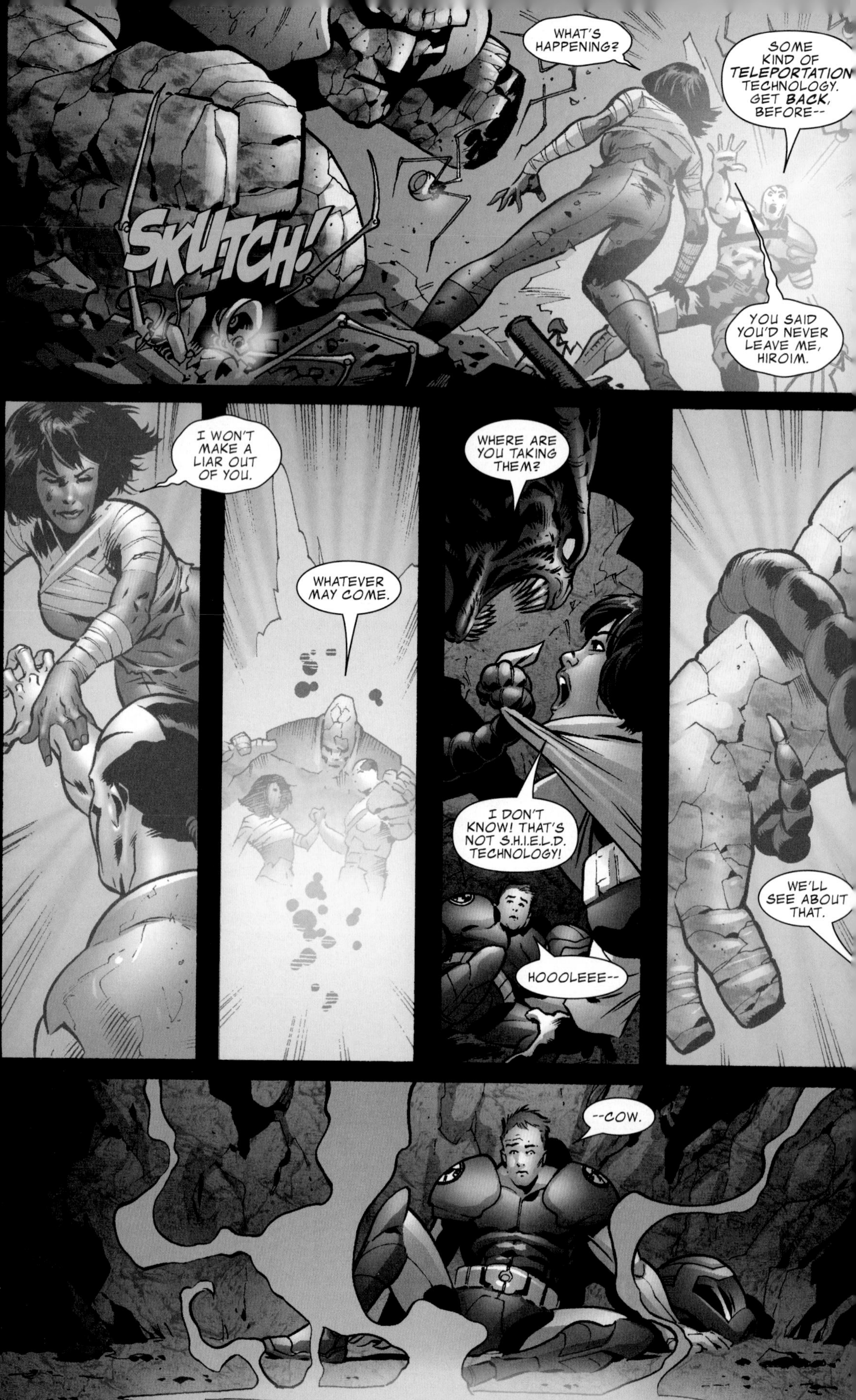
WHAT'S HAPPENING?
SOME KIND OF TELEPORTATION TECHNOLOGY. GET BACK, BEFORE--
SKUTCH!
YOU SAID YOU'D NEVER LEAVE ME, HIROIM.
I WON'T MAKE A LIAR OUT OF YOU.
WHATEVER MAY COME.
WHERE ARE YOU TAKING THEM?
I DON'T KNOW! THAT'S NOT S.H.I.E.L.D. TECHNOLOGY!
HOOOLEEE--
WE'LL SEE ABOUT THAT.
--COW.

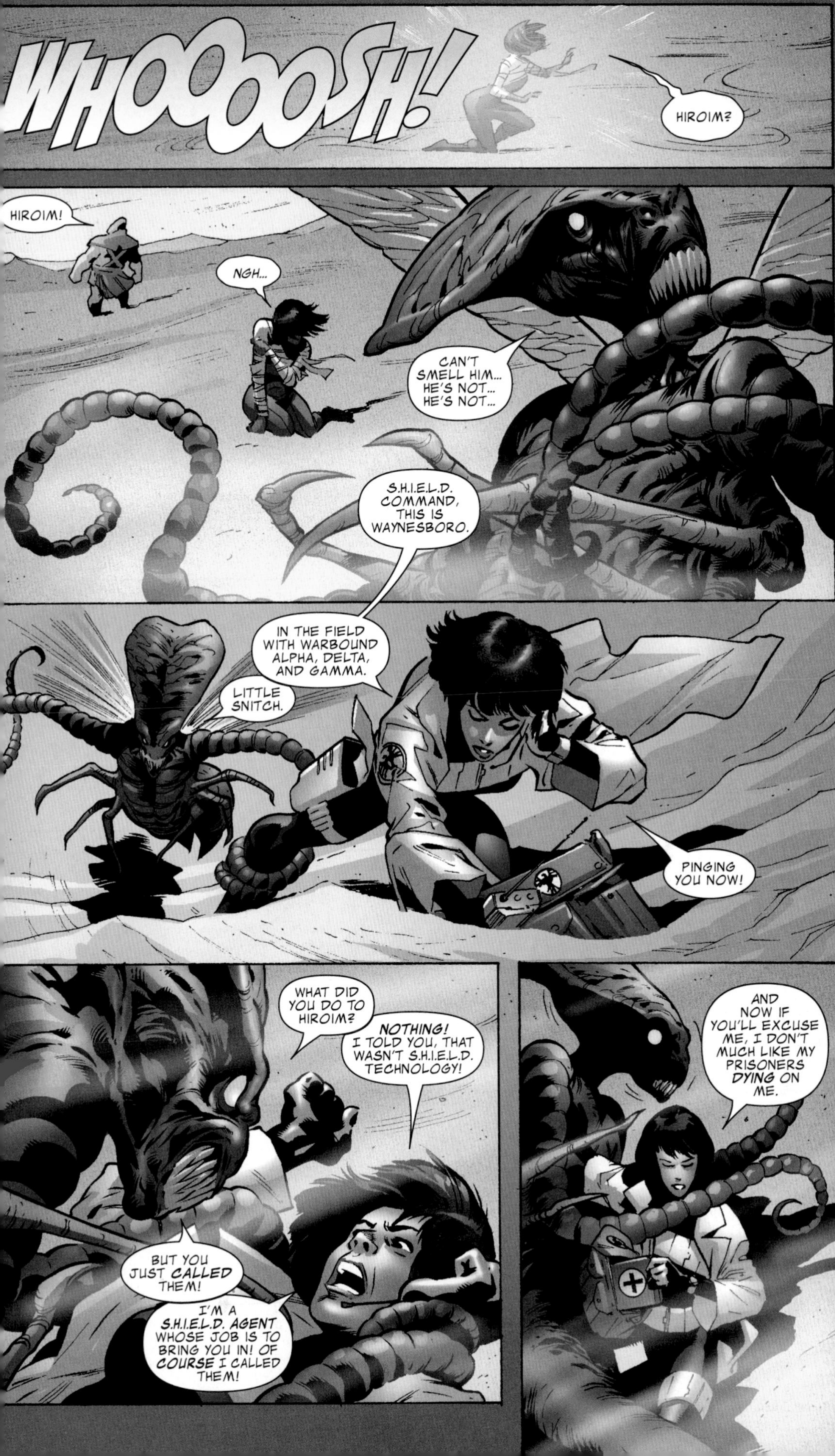
WHOOOOOSH!
HIROIM?
HIROIM!
NGH...
CAN'T SMELL HIM... HE'S NOT... HE'S NOT...
S.H.I.E.L.D. COMMAND, THIS IS WAYNESBORO.
IN THE FIELD WITH WARBOUND ALPHA, DELTA, AND GAMMA.
LITTLE SNITCH.
PINGING YOU NOW!
WHAT DID YOU DO TO HIROIM?
NOTHING! I TOLD YOU, THAT WASN'T S.H.I.E.L.D. TECHNOLOGY!
BUT YOU JUST CALLED THEM!
I'M A S.H.I.E.L.D. AGENT WHOSE JOB IS TO BRING YOU IN! OF COURSE I CALLED THEM!
AND NOW IF YOU'LL EXCUSE ME, I DON'T MUCH LIKE MY PRISONERS DYING ON ME.

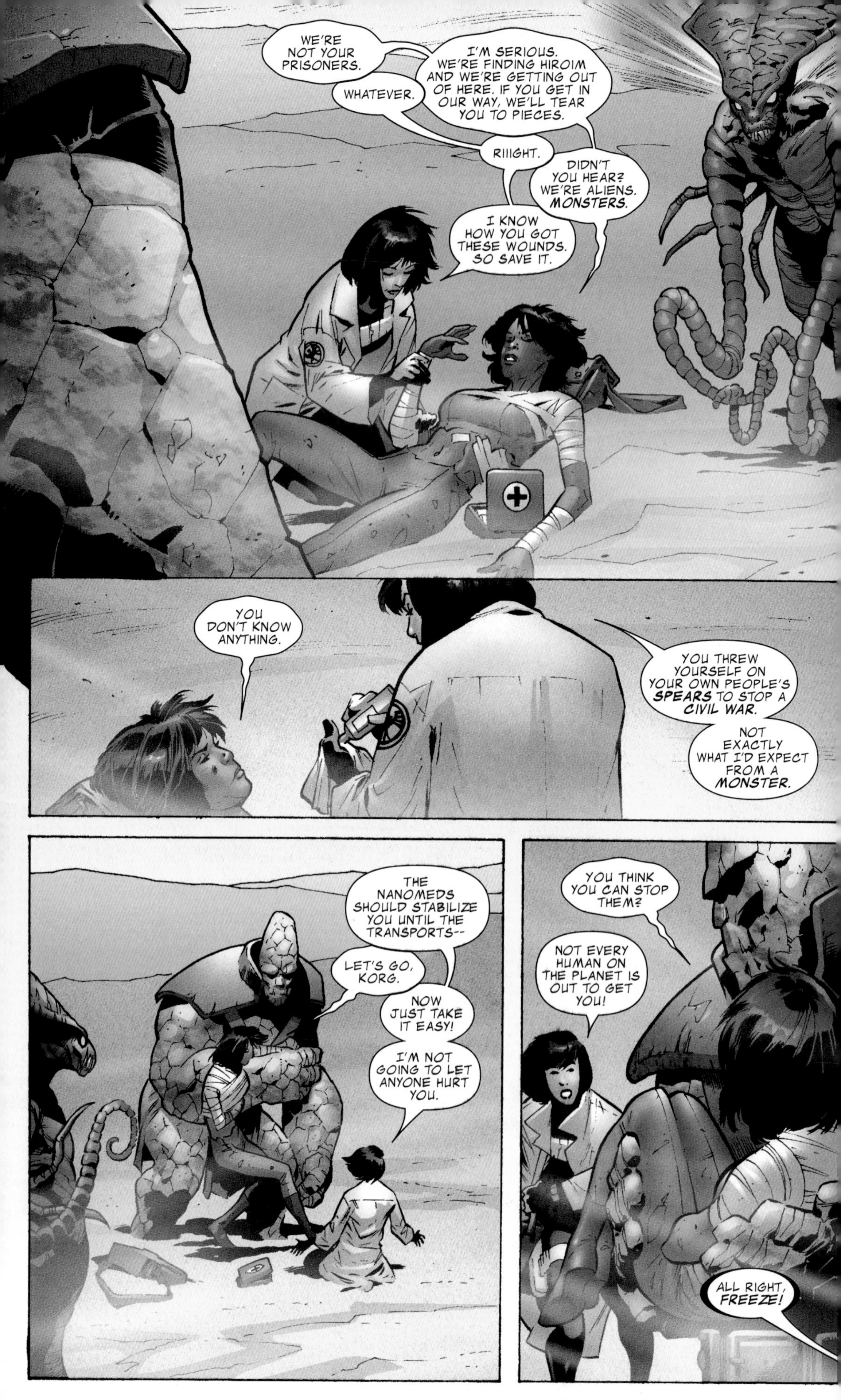
WE'RE NOT YOUR PRISONERS.
I'M SERIOUS. WE'RE FINDING HIROIM AND WE'RE GETTING OUT OF HERE. IF YOU GET IN OUR WAY, WE'LL TEAR YOU TO PIECES.
WHATEVER.
RIIIGHT.
DIDN'T YOU HEAR? WE'RE ALIENS. MONSTERS.
I KNOW HOW YOU GOT THESE WOUNDS. SO SAVE IT.
YOU DON'T KNOW ANYTHING.
YOU THREW YOURSELF ON YOUR OWN PEOPLE'S SPEARS TO STOP A CIVIL WAR.
NOT EXACTLY WHAT I'D EXPECT FROM A MONSTER.
THE NANOMEDS SHOULD STABILIZE YOU UNTIL THE TRANSPORTS--
LET'S GO, KORG.
NOW JUST TAKE IT EASY!
I'M NOT GOING TO LET ANYONE HURT YOU.
YOU THINK YOU CAN STOP THEM?
NOT EVERY HUMAN ON THE PLANET IS OUT TO GET YOU!
ALL RIGHT, FREEZE!

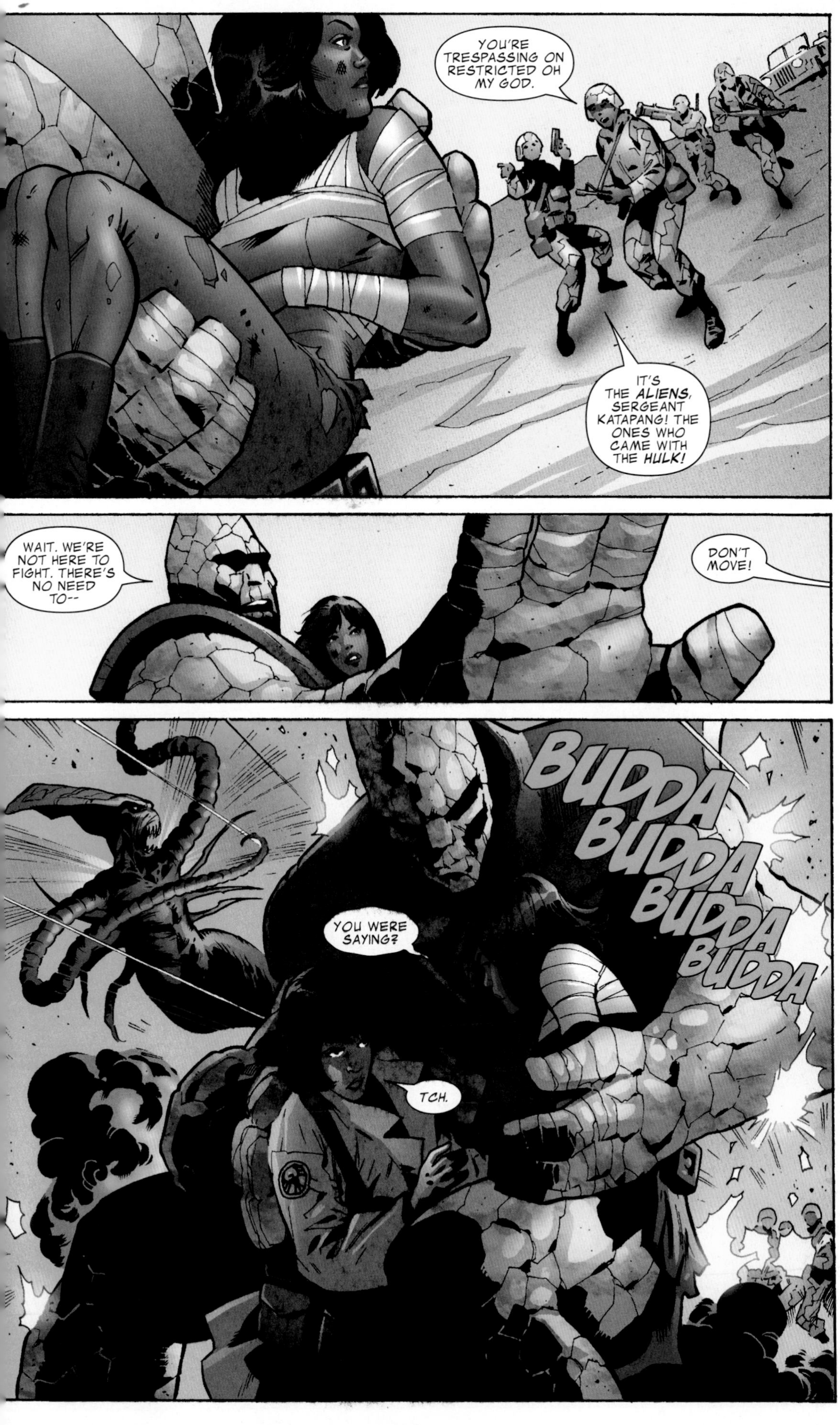
YOU'RE TRESPASSING ON RESTRICTED OH MY GOD.
IT'S THE ALIENS, SERGEANT KATAPANG! THE ONES WHO CAME WITH THE HULK!
WAIT. WE'RE NOT HERE TO FIGHT. THERE'S NO NEED TO--
DON'T MOVE!
BUDDA BUDDA BUDDA BUDDA
YOU WERE SAYING?
TCH.

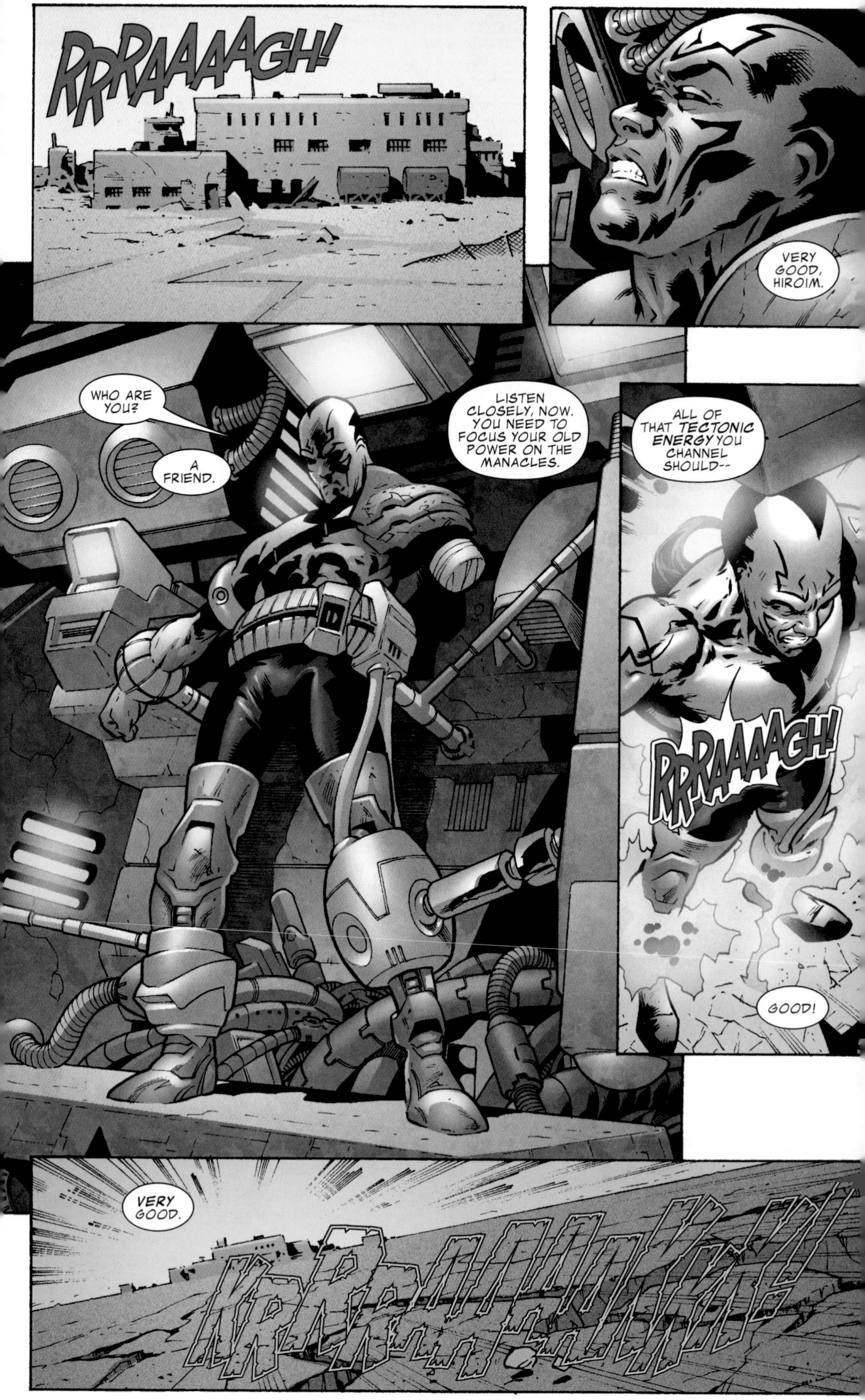
RRRAAAAGH!
VERY GOOD, HIROIM.
WHO ARE YOU?
A FRIEND.
LISTEN CLOSELY, NOW. YOU NEED TO FOCUS YOUR OLD POWER ON THE MANACLES.
ALL OF THAT TECTONIC ENERGY YOU CHANNEL SHOULD--
RRRAAAAGH!
GOOD!
VERY GOOD.

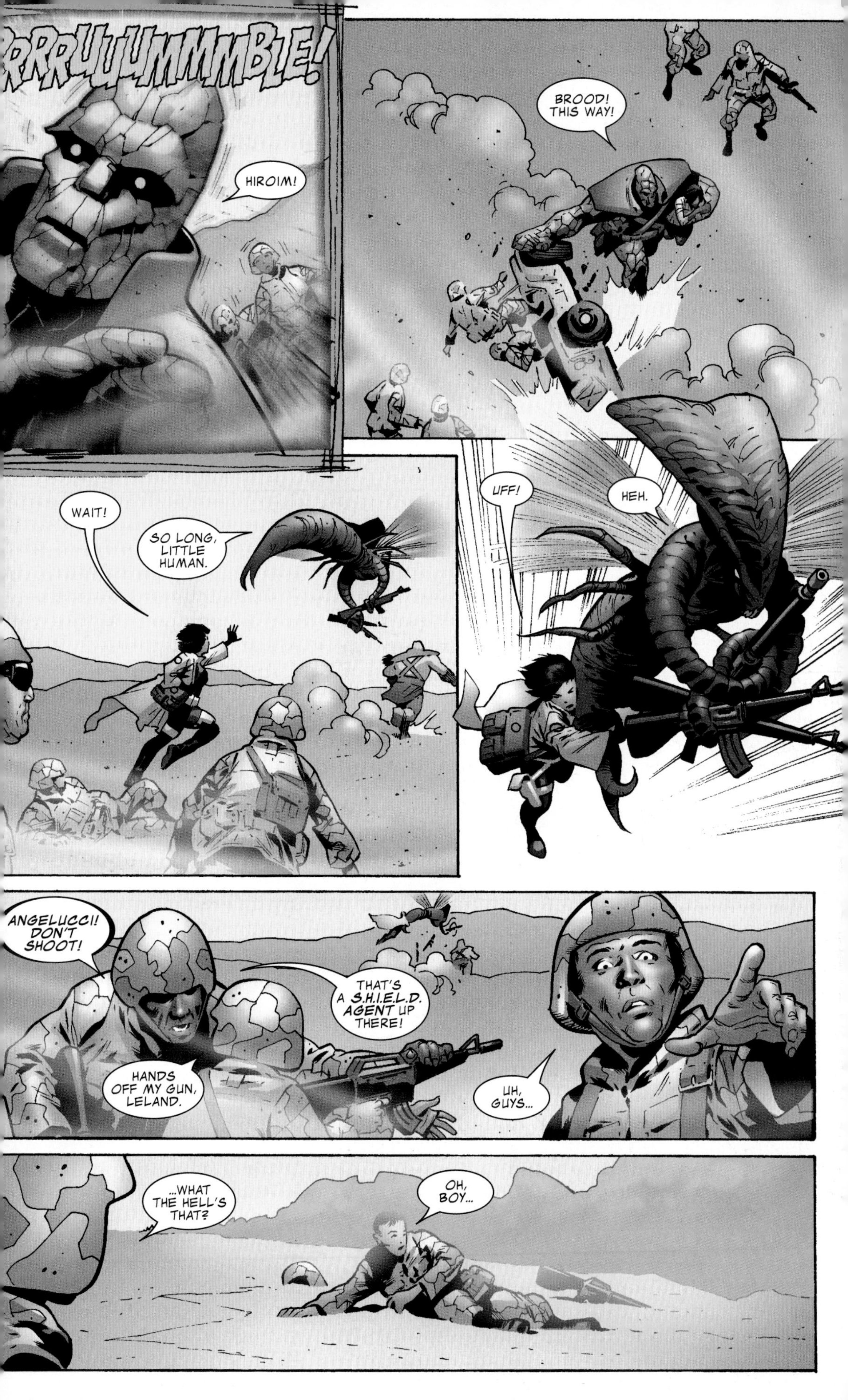
RRRUUUMMMBLE!
HIROIM!
BROOD! THIS WAY!
WAIT!
SO LONG, LITTLE HUMAN.
UFF!
HEH.
ANGELUCCI! DON'T SHOOT!
THAT'S A S.H.I.E.L.D. AGENT UP THERE!
HANDS OFF MY GUN, LELAND.
UH, GUYS...
...WHAT THE HELL'S THAT?
OH, BOY...

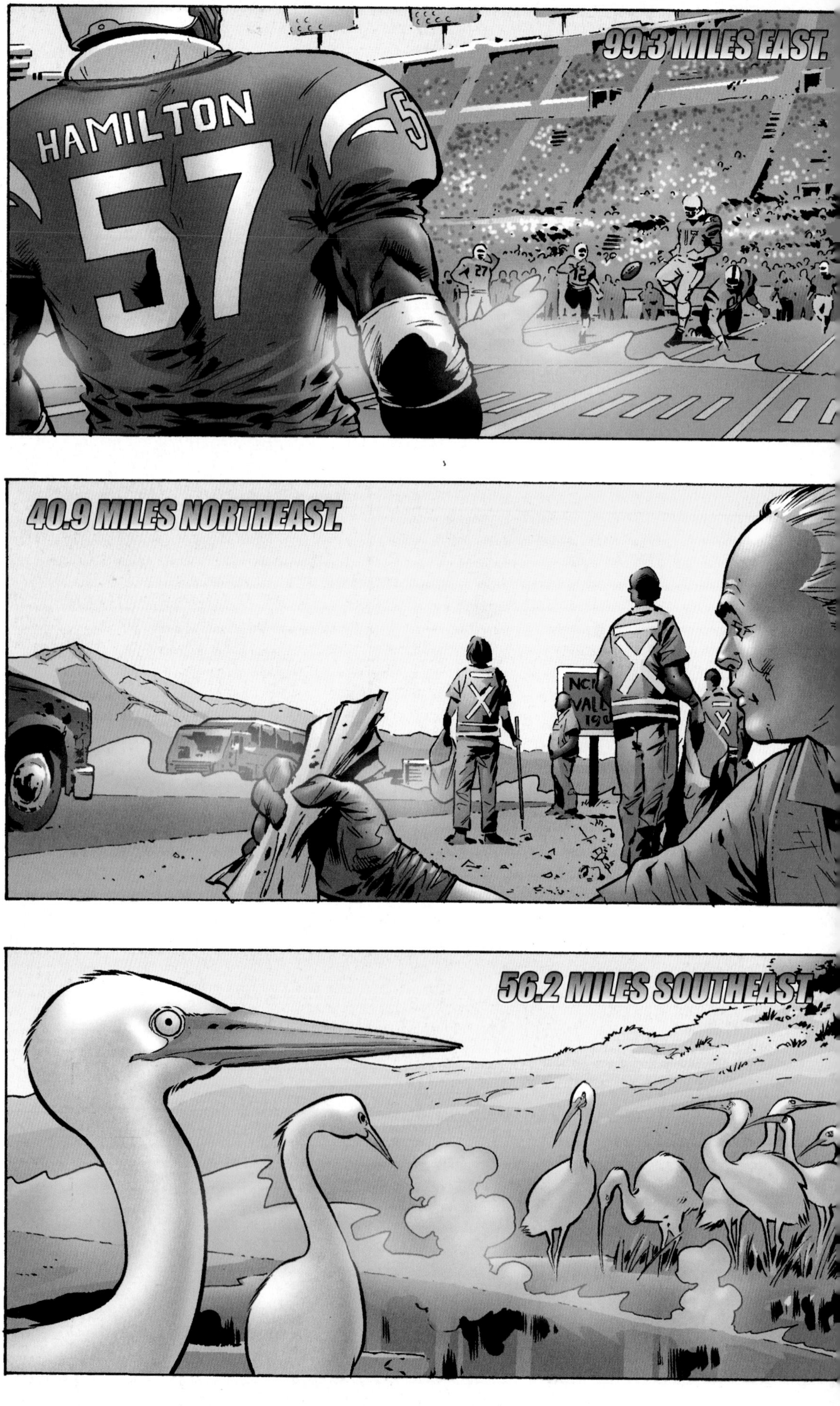

99.3 MILES EAST.
HAMILTON
57
40.9 MILES NORTHEAST.
56.2 MILES SOUTHEAST.

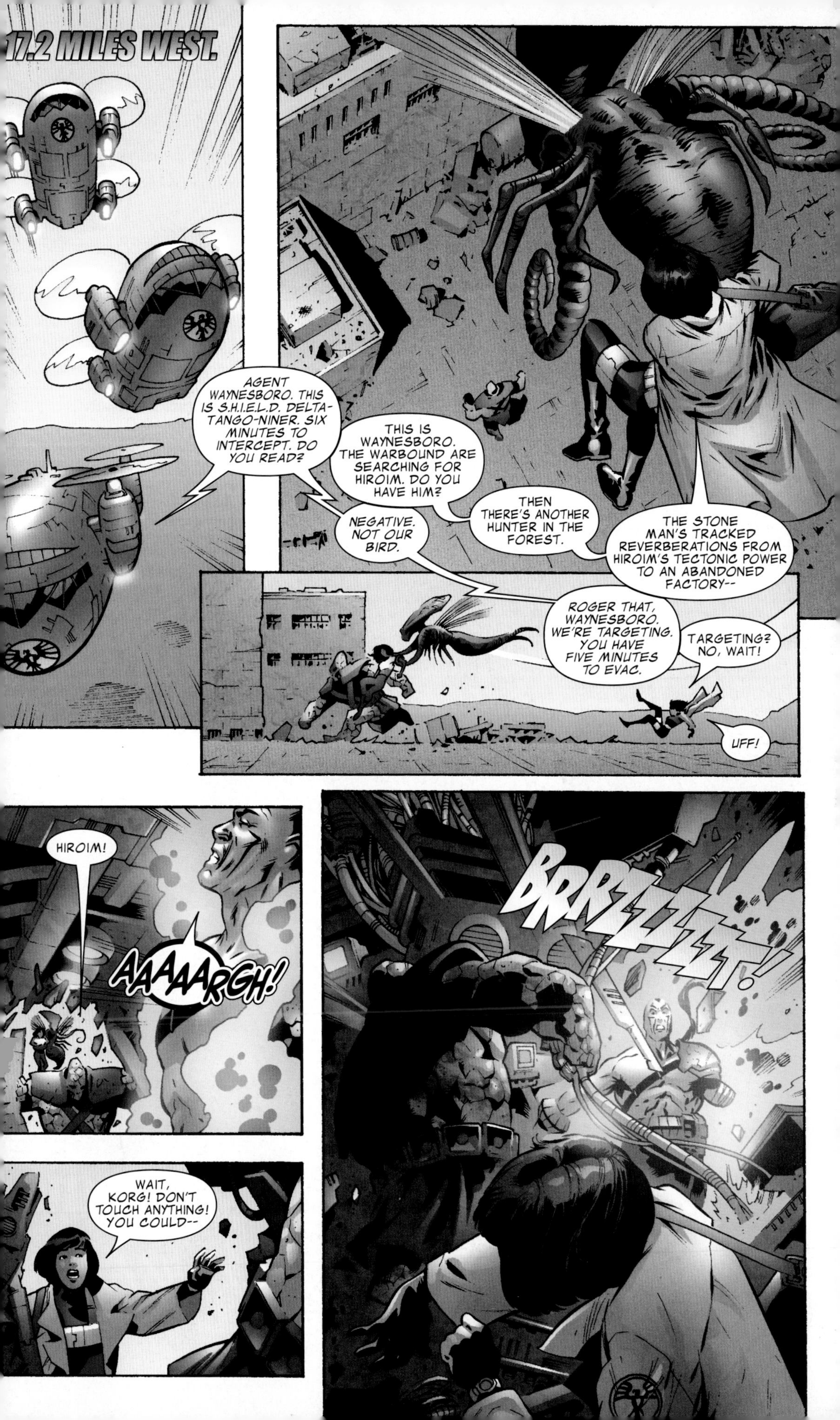
17.2 MILES WEST.
AGENT WAYNESBORO. THIS IS S.H.I.E.L.D. DELTA-TANGO-NINER. SIX MINUTES TO INTERCEPT. DO YOU READ?
THIS IS WAYNESBORO. THE WARBOUND ARE SEARCHING FOR HIROIM. DO YOU HAVE HIM?
NEGATIVE. NOT OUR BIRD.
THEN THERE'S ANOTHER HUNTER IN THE FOREST.
THE STONE MAN'S TRACKED REVERBERATIONS FROM HIROIM'S TECTONIC POWER TO AN ABANDONED FACTORY--
ROGER THAT, WAYNESBORO. WE'RE TARGETING. YOU HAVE FIVE MINUTES TO EVAC.
TARGETING? NO, WAIT!
UFF!
HIROIM!
AAAAARGH!
WAIT, KORG! DON'T TOUCH ANYTHING! YOU COULD--
BRRZZZT!

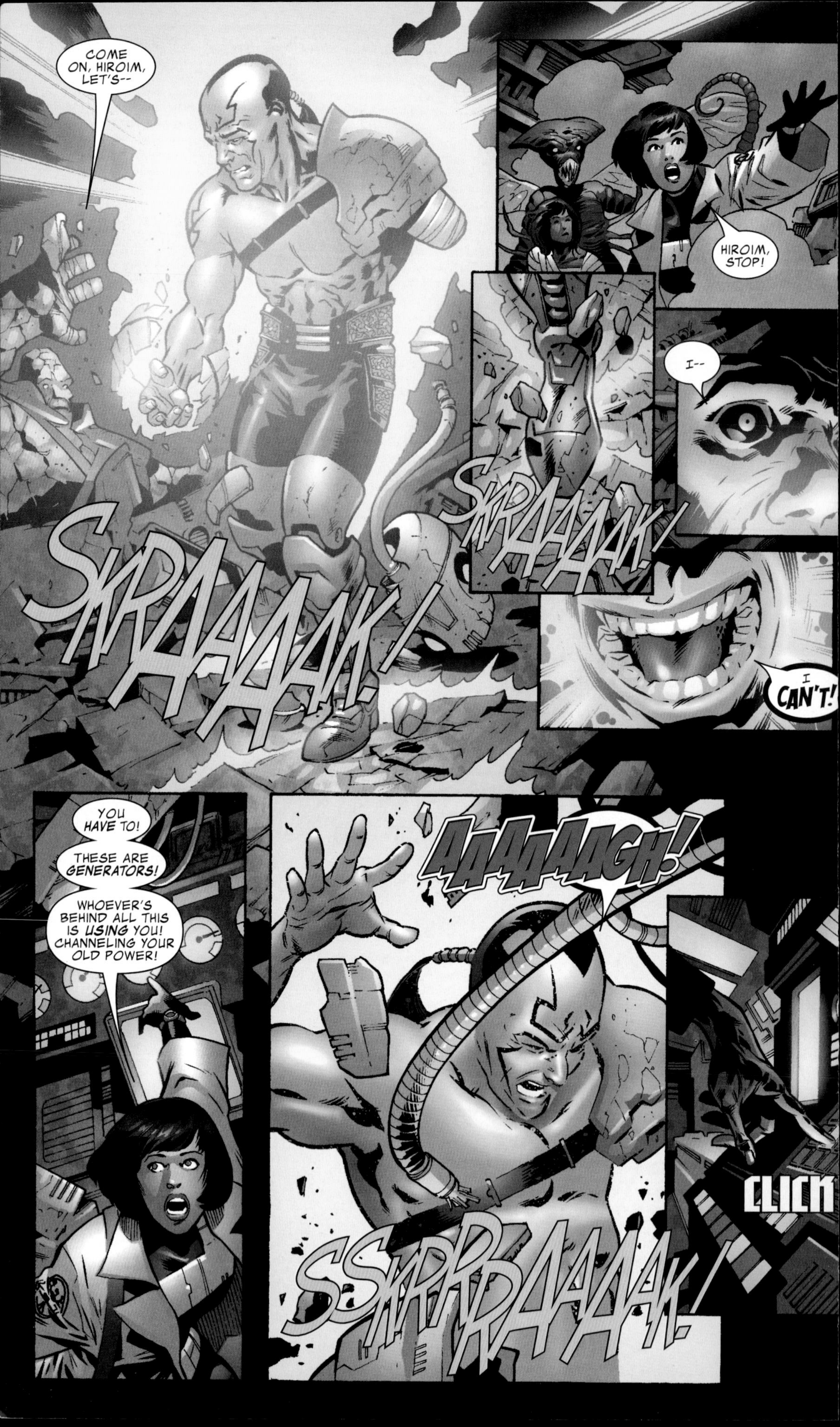
COME ON, HIROIM, LET'S--
HIROIM, STOP!
SKRAAAAK!
SKRAAAAAK!
I--
I CAN'T!
YOU HAVE TO!
THESE ARE GENERATORS!
WHOEVER'S BEHIND ALL THIS IS USING YOU! CHANNELING YOUR OLD POWER!
AAAAAAGH!
SSKRRAAAAK!
CLICK

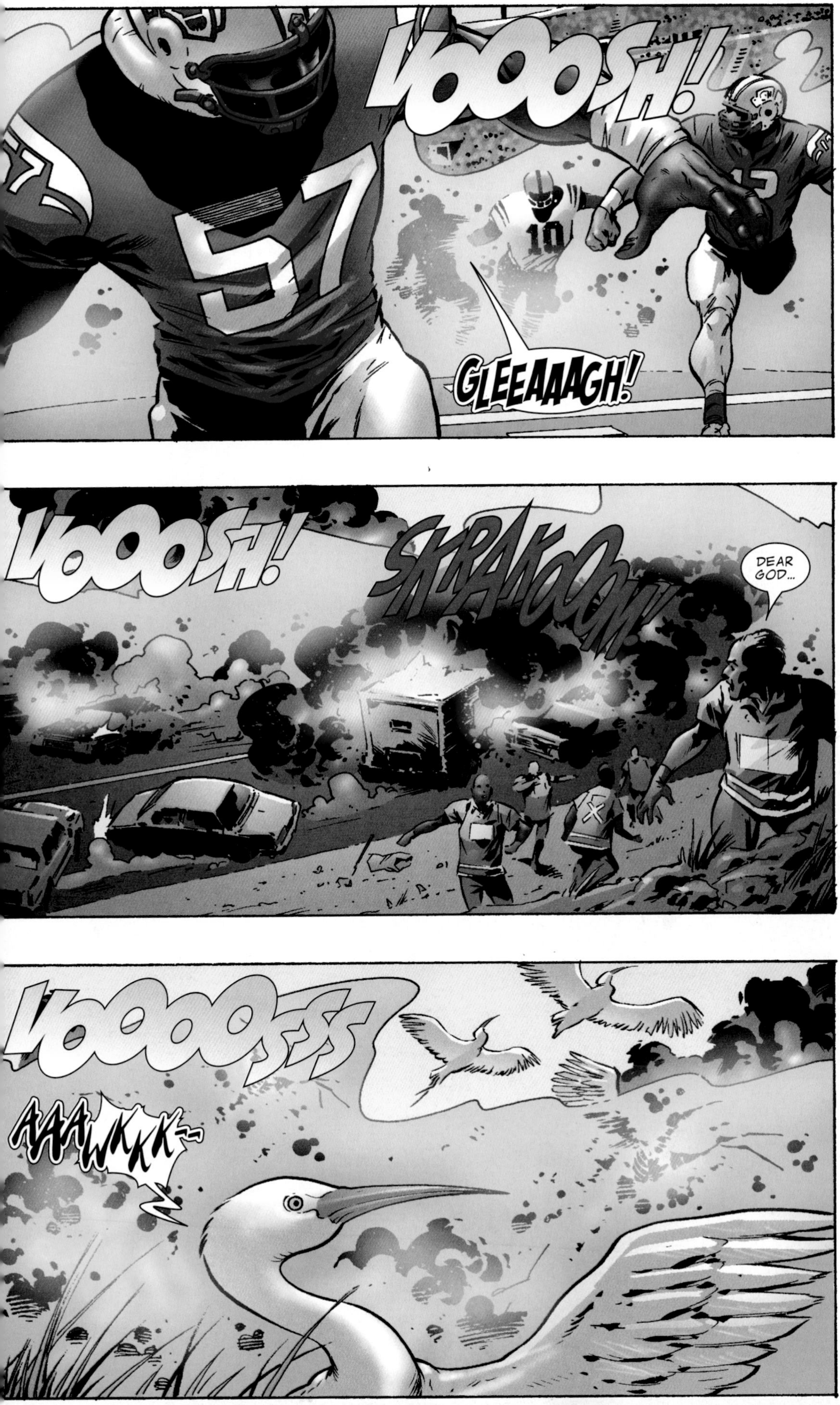
VOOOSH!
GLEEAAAGH!
VOOOSH!
SKRAKOOOM!
DEAR GOD...
VOOOOFSS
AAAWKKK--

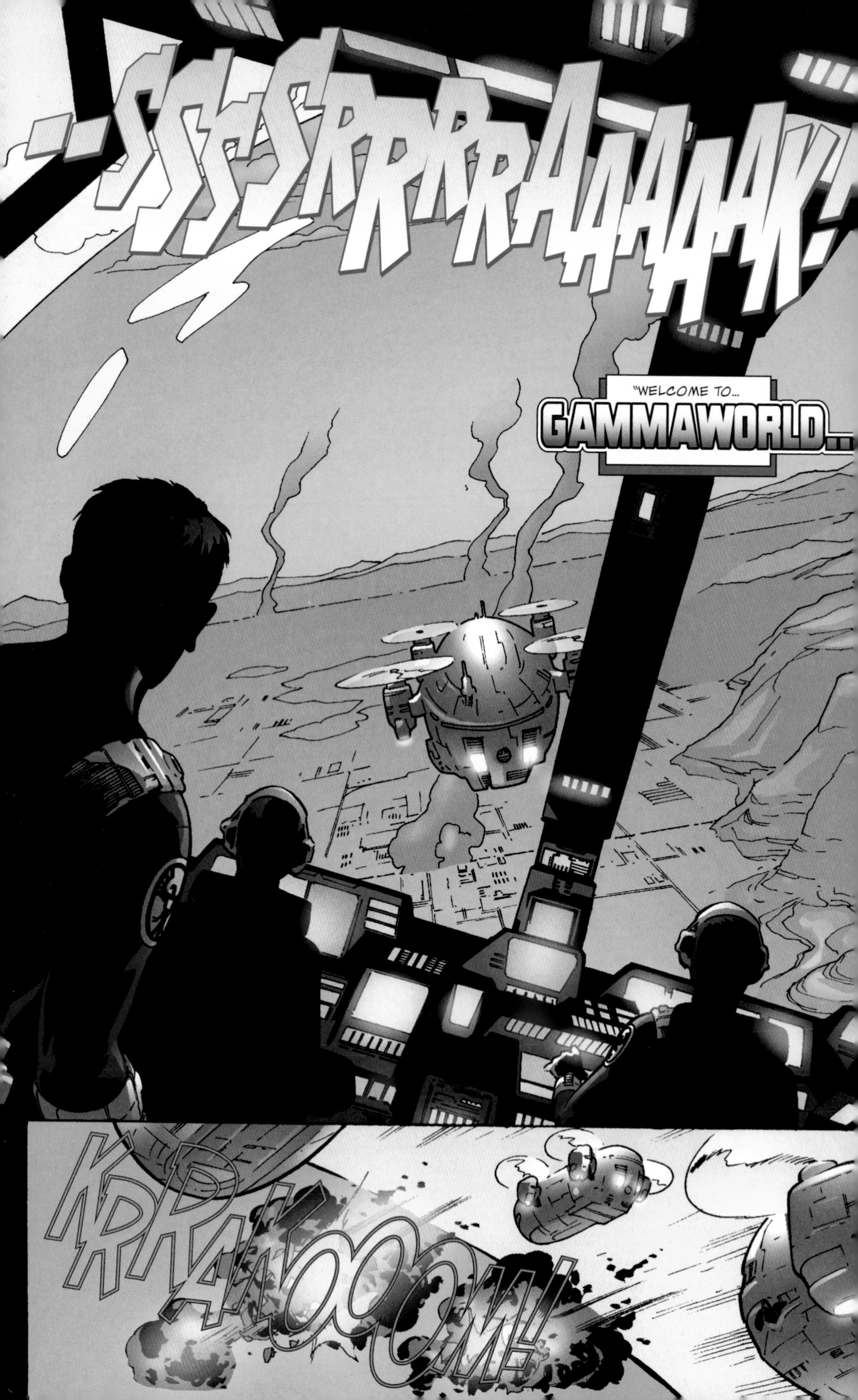
--SSSSRRRRAAAAAK!
"WELCOME TO...
GAMMAWORLD...
KRAKOOOM!

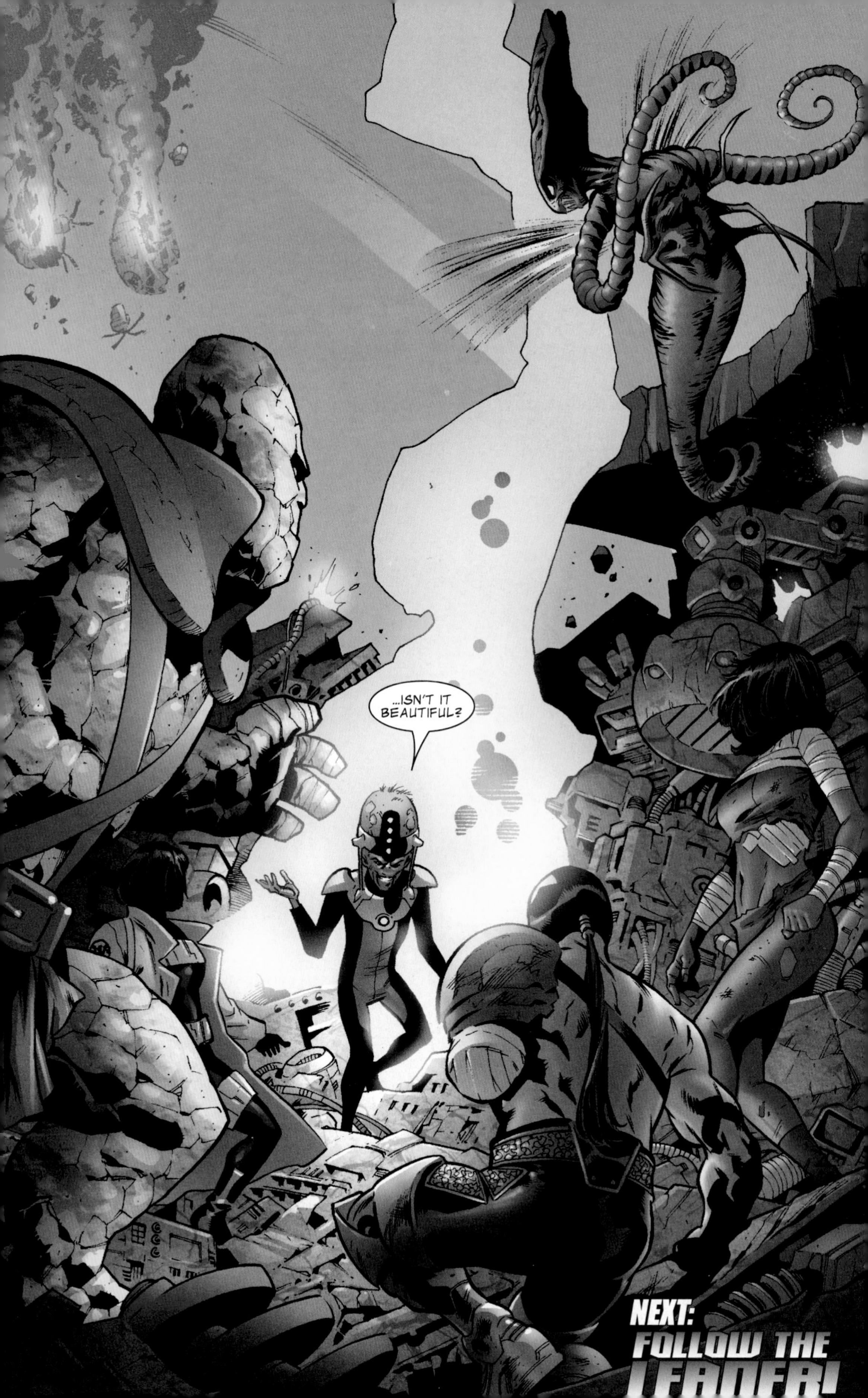
...ISN'T IT BEAUTIFUL?
NEXT:
FOLLOW THE

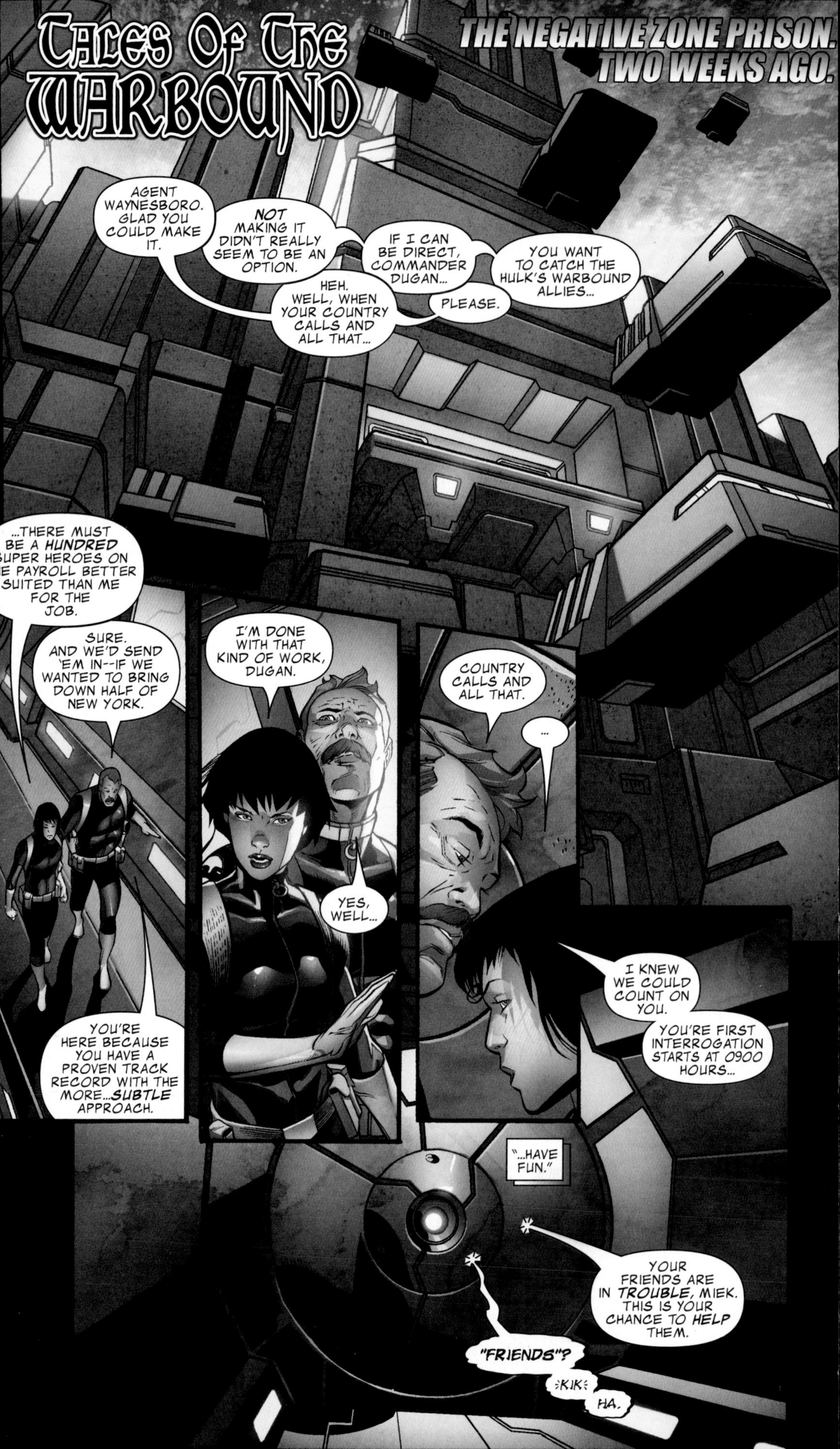
TALES OF THE WARBOUND
THE NEGATIVE ZONE PRISON. TWO WEEKS AGO.
AGENT WAYNESBORO. GLAD YOU COULD MAKE IT.
NOT MAKING IT DIDN'T REALLY SEEM TO BE AN OPTION.
HEH. WELL, WHEN YOUR COUNTRY CALLS AND ALL THAT...
IF I CAN BE DIRECT, COMMANDER DUGAN...
PLEASE.
YOU WANT TO CATCH THE HULK'S WARBOUND ALLIES...
...THERE MUST BE A HUNDRED SUPER HEROES ON THE PAYROLL BETTER SUITED THAN ME FOR THE JOB.
SURE. AND WE'D SEND 'EM IN--IF WE WANTED TO BRING DOWN HALF OF NEW YORK.
YOU'RE HERE BECAUSE YOU HAVE A PROVEN TRACK RECORD WITH THE MORE...SUBTLE APPROACH.
I'M DONE WITH THAT KIND OF WORK, DUGAN.
YES, WELL...
COUNTRY CALLS AND ALL THAT.
...
I KNEW WE COULD COUNT ON YOU.
YOU'RE FIRST INTERROGATION STARTS AT 0900 HOURS...
"...HAVE FUN."
YOUR FRIENDS ARE IN TROUBLE, MIEK. THIS IS YOUR CHANCE TO HELP THEM.
"FRIENDS"?
KIK
HA.

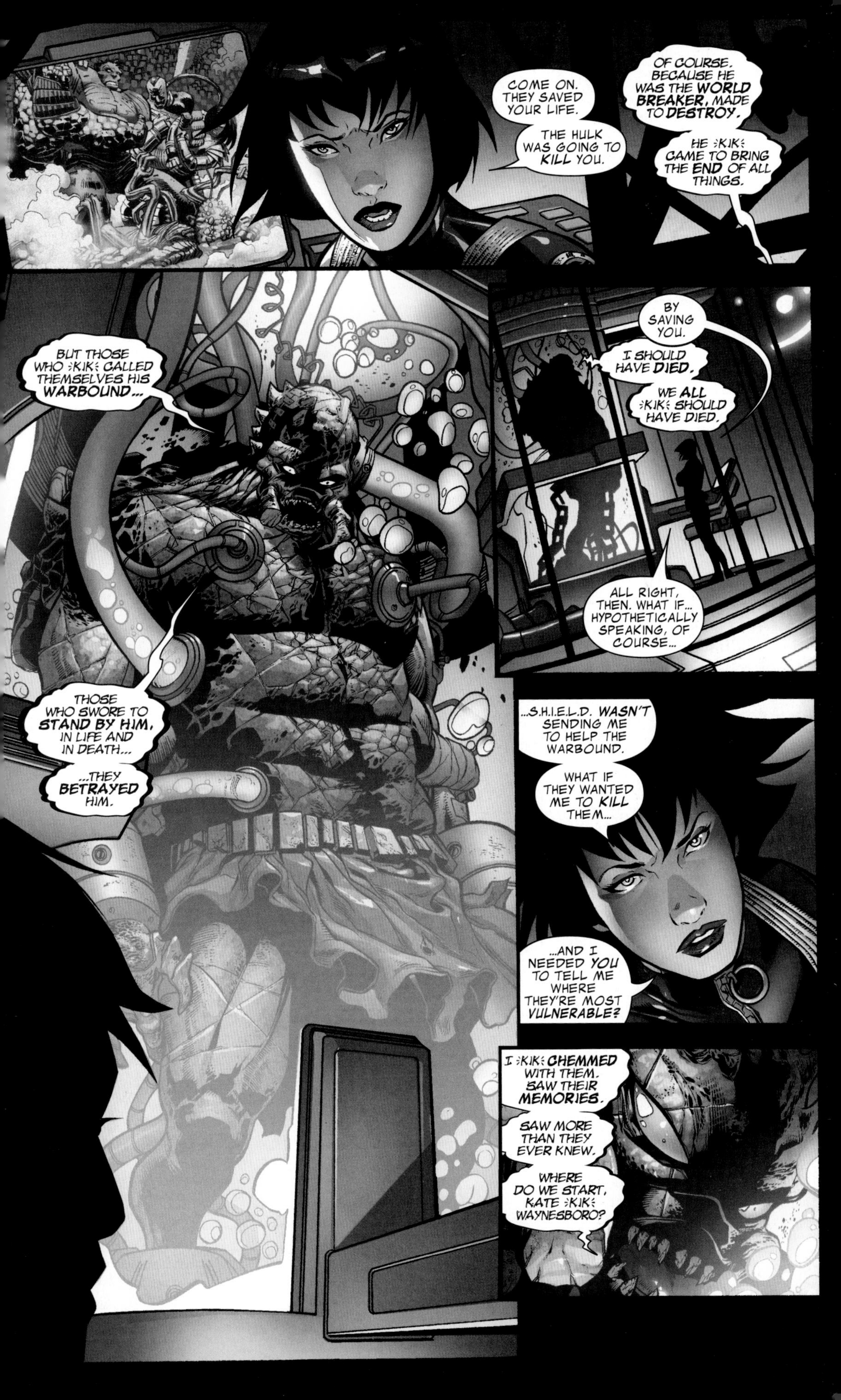

COME ON. THEY SAVED YOUR LIFE.
THE HULK WAS GOING TO KILL YOU.
OF COURSE. BECAUSE HE WAS THE WORLD BREAKER, MADE TO DESTROY.
HE ⁝KIK⁝ CAME TO BRING THE END OF ALL THINGS.
BUT THOSE WHO ⁝KIK⁝ CALLED THEMSELVES HIS WARBOUND...
THOSE WHO SWORE TO STAND BY HIM, IN LIFE AND IN DEATH...
...THEY BETRAYED HIM.
BY SAVING YOU.
I SHOULD HAVE DIED.
WE ALL ⁝KIK⁝ SHOULD HAVE DIED.
ALL RIGHT, THEN. WHAT IF... HYPOTHETICALLY SPEAKING, OF COURSE...
...S.H.I.E.L.D. WASN'T SENDING ME TO HELP THE WARBOUND.
WHAT IF THEY WANTED ME TO KILL THEM...
...AND I NEEDED YOU TO TELL ME WHERE THEY'RE MOST VULNERABLE?
I ⁝KIK⁝ CHEMMED WITH THEM. SAW THEIR MEMORIES.
SAW MORE THAN THEY EVER KNEW.
WHERE DO WE START, KATE ⁝KIK⁝ WAYNESBORO?

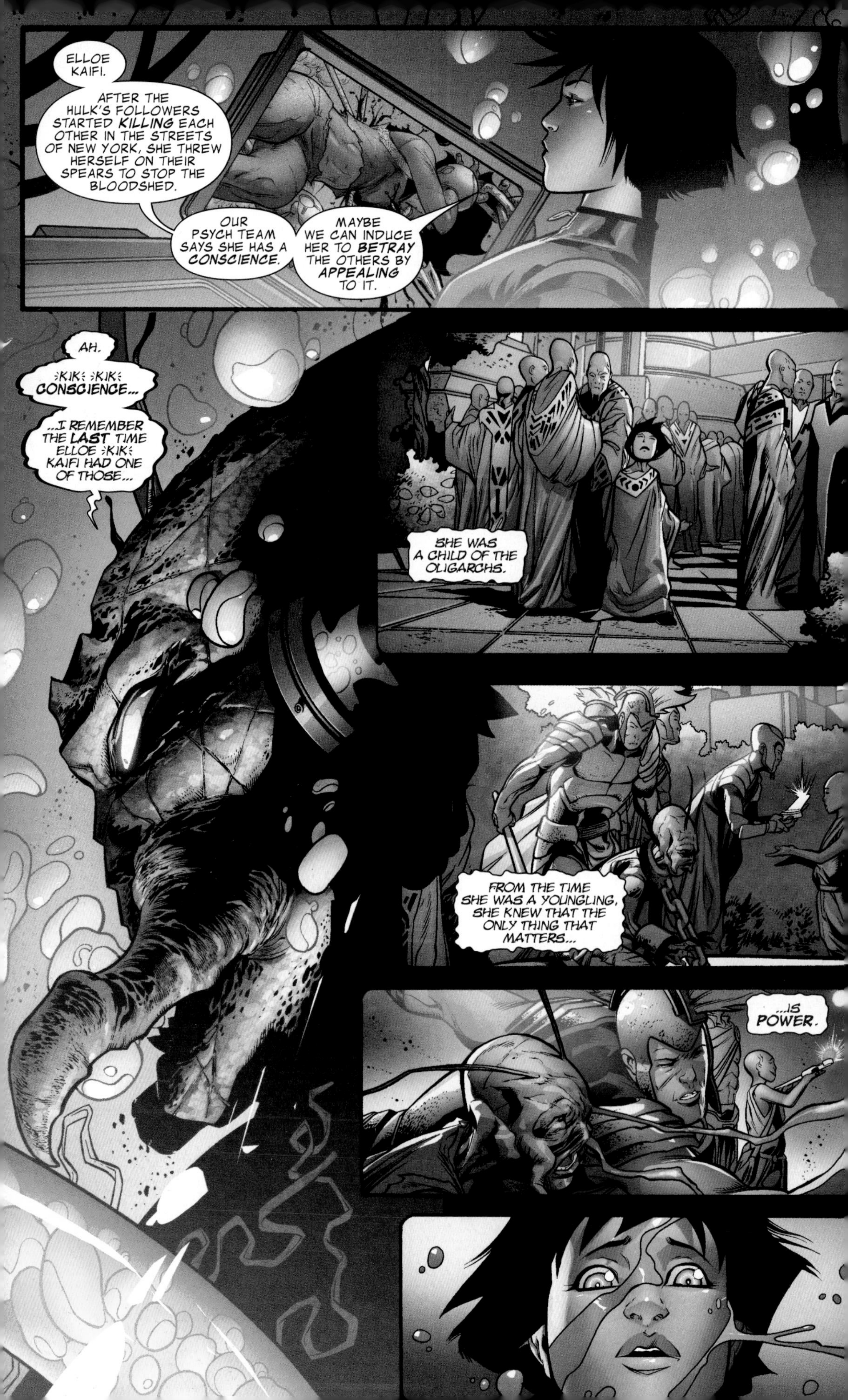

ELLOE KAIFI.
AFTER THE HULK'S FOLLOWERS STARTED KILLING EACH OTHER IN THE STREETS OF NEW YORK, SHE THREW HERSELF ON THEIR SPEARS TO STOP THE BLOODSHED.
OUR PSYCH TEAM SAYS SHE HAS A CONSCIENCE.
MAYBE WE CAN INDUCE HER TO BETRAY THE OTHERS BY APPEALING TO IT.
AH.
KIK KIK CONSCIENCE...
...I REMEMBER THE LAST TIME ELLOE KIK KAIFI HAD ONE OF THOSE...
SHE WAS A CHILD OF THE OLIGARCHS.
FROM THE TIME SHE WAS A YOUNGLING, SHE KNEW THAT THE ONLY THING THAT MATTERS...
...IS POWER.

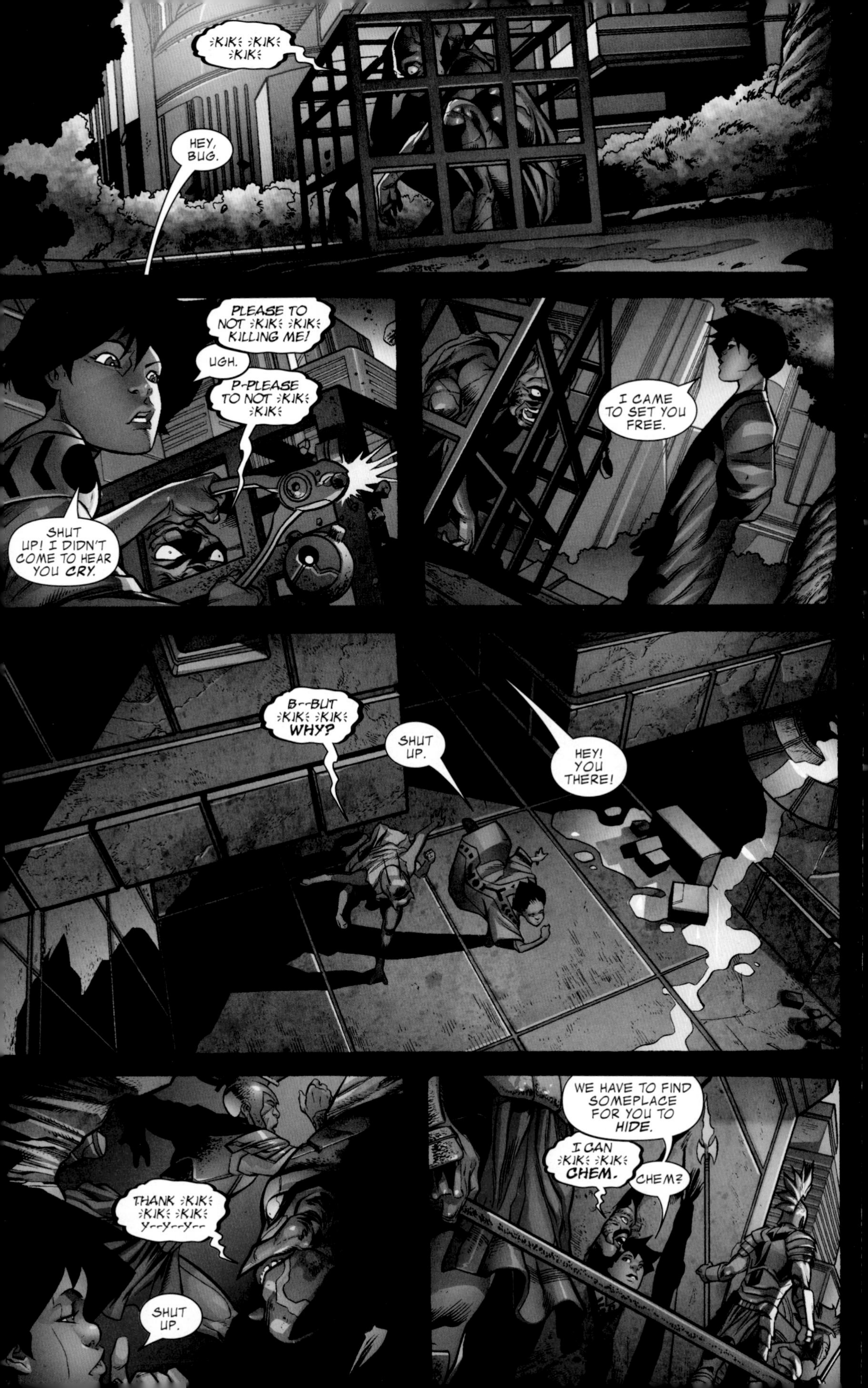

⁝KIK⁝ ⁝KIK⁝ ⁝KIK⁝
HEY, BUG.
PLEASE TO NOT ⁝KIK⁝ ⁝KIK⁝ KILLING ME!
UGH.
P-PLEASE TO NOT ⁝KIK⁝ ⁝KIK⁝
SHUT UP! I DIDN'T COME TO HEAR YOU **CRY**.
I CAME TO SET YOU FREE.
B--BUT ⁝KIK⁝ ⁝KIK⁝ **WHY?**
SHUT UP.
HEY! YOU THERE!
THANK ⁝KIK⁝ ⁝KIK⁝ ⁝KIK⁝ Y--Y--Y--
SHUT UP.
WE HAVE TO FIND SOMEPLACE FOR YOU TO **HIDE**.
I CAN ⁝KIK⁝ ⁝KIK⁝ **CHEM.**
CHEM?

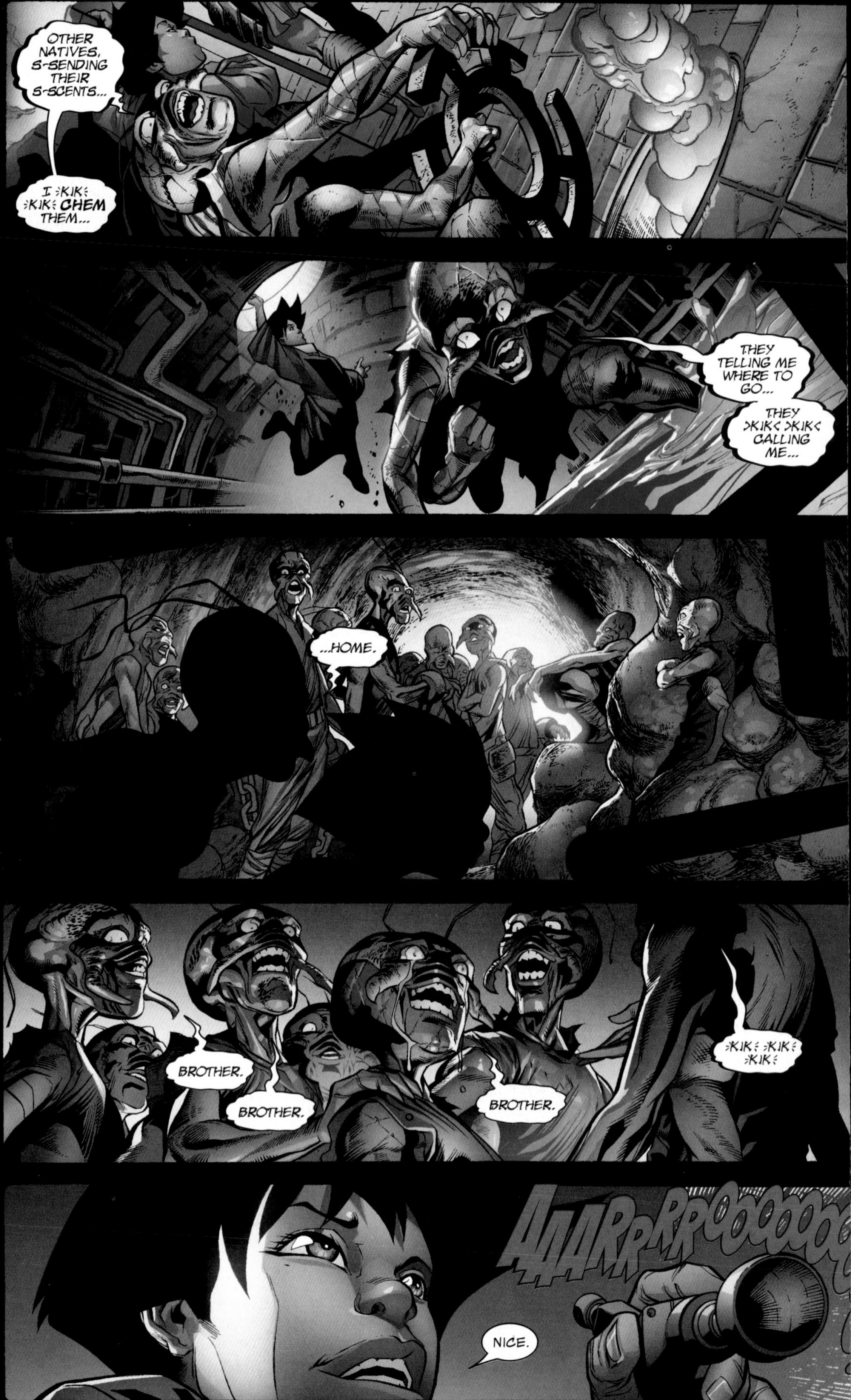
OTHER NATIVES, S-SENDING THEIR S-SCENTS...
I >KIK< >KIK< CHEM THEM...
THEY TELLING ME WHERE TO GO...
THEY >KIK< >KIK< CALLING ME...
...HOME.
BROTHER.
BROTHER.
BROTHER.
>KIK< >KIK< >KIK<
AAARRRROOOOOO
NICE.

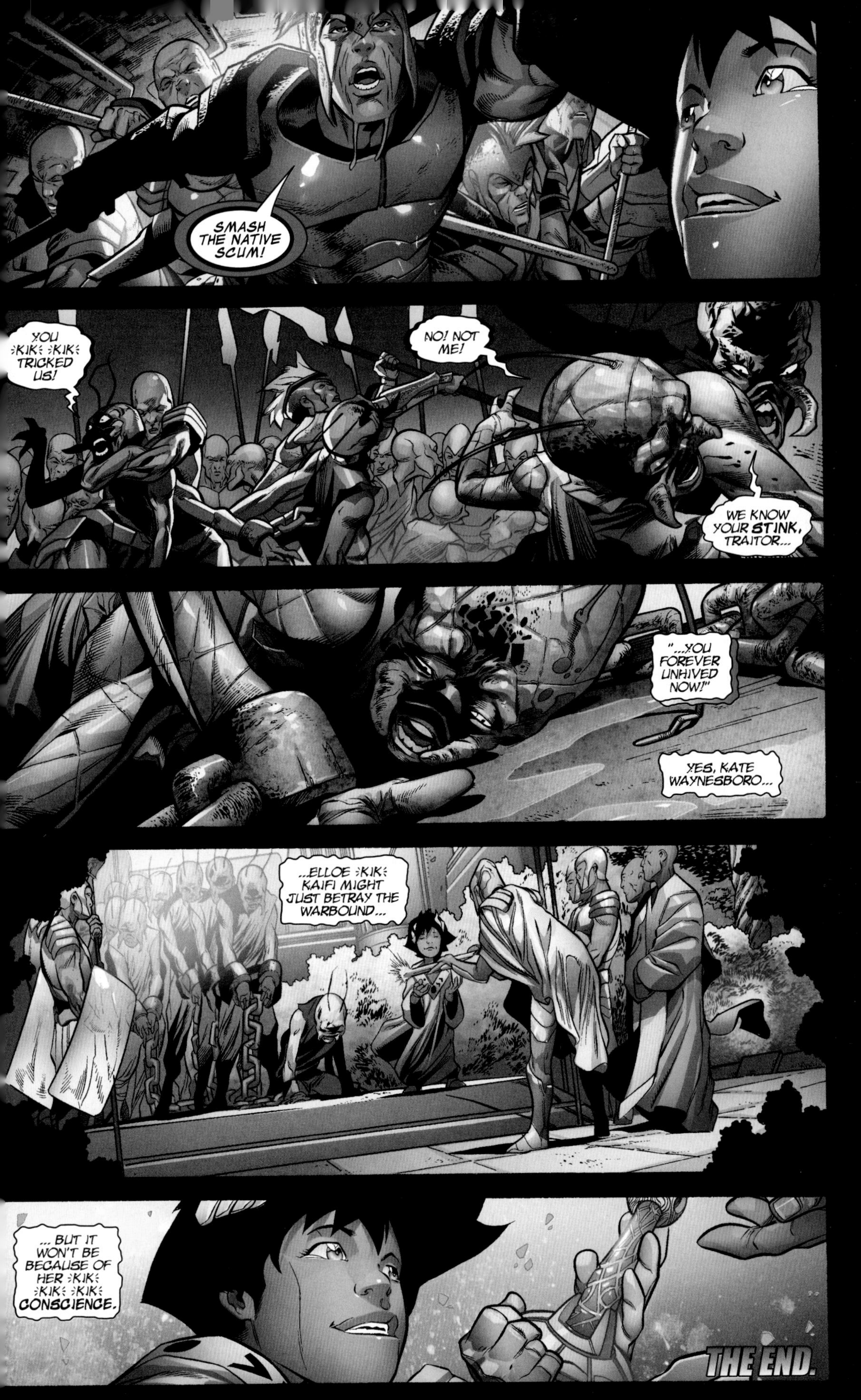
SMASH THE NATIVE SCUM!
YOU ⋗KIK⋖ ⋗KIK⋖ TRICKED US!
NO! NOT ME!
WE KNOW YOUR STINK, TRAITOR...
"...YOU FOREVER UNHIVED NOW!"
YES, KATE WAYNESBORO...
...ELLOE ⋗KIK⋖ KAIFI MIGHT JUST BETRAY THE WARBOUND...
... BUT IT WON'T BE BECAUSE OF HER ⋗KIK⋖ ⋗KIK⋖ ⋗KIK⋖ CONSCIENCE.
THE END.

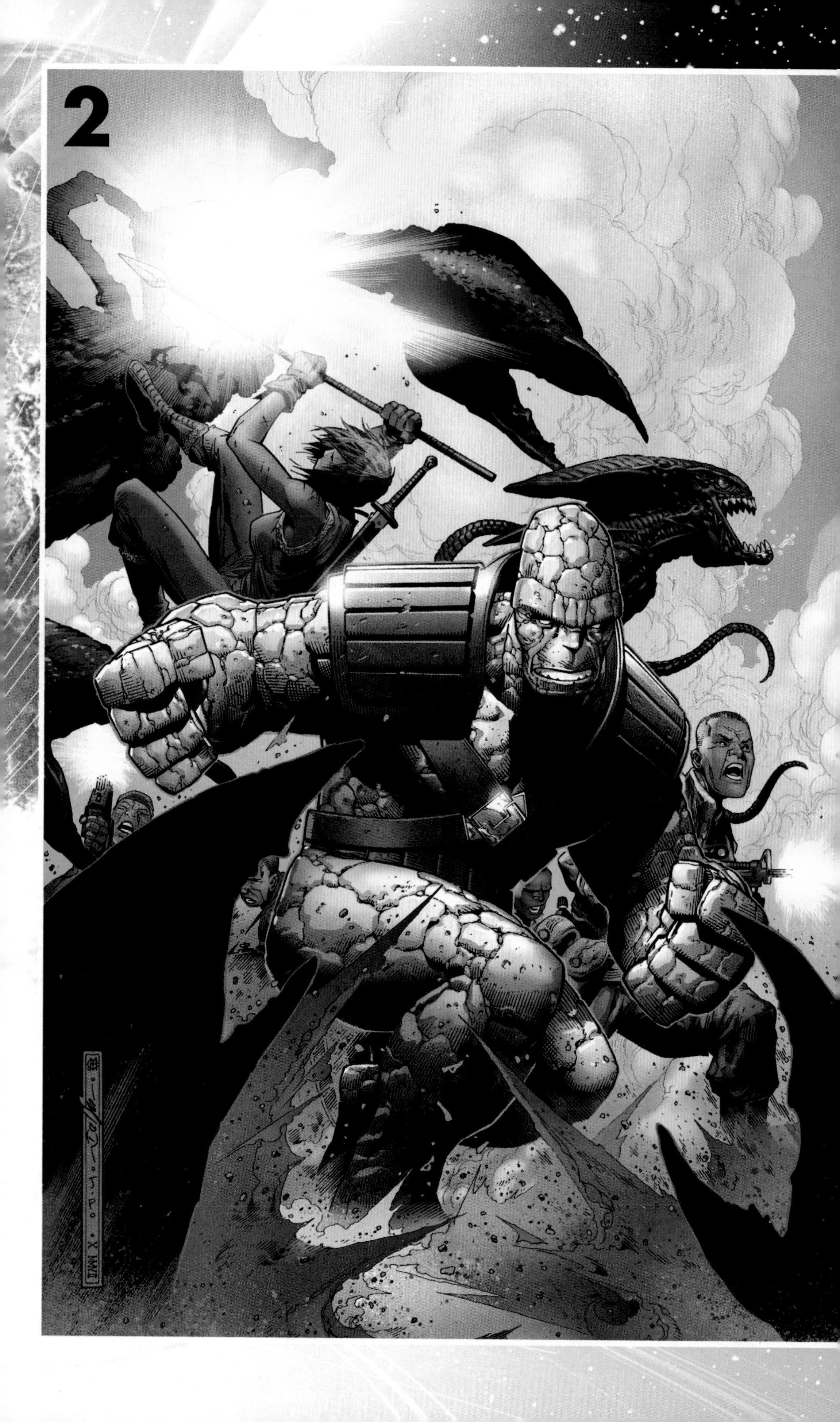
2

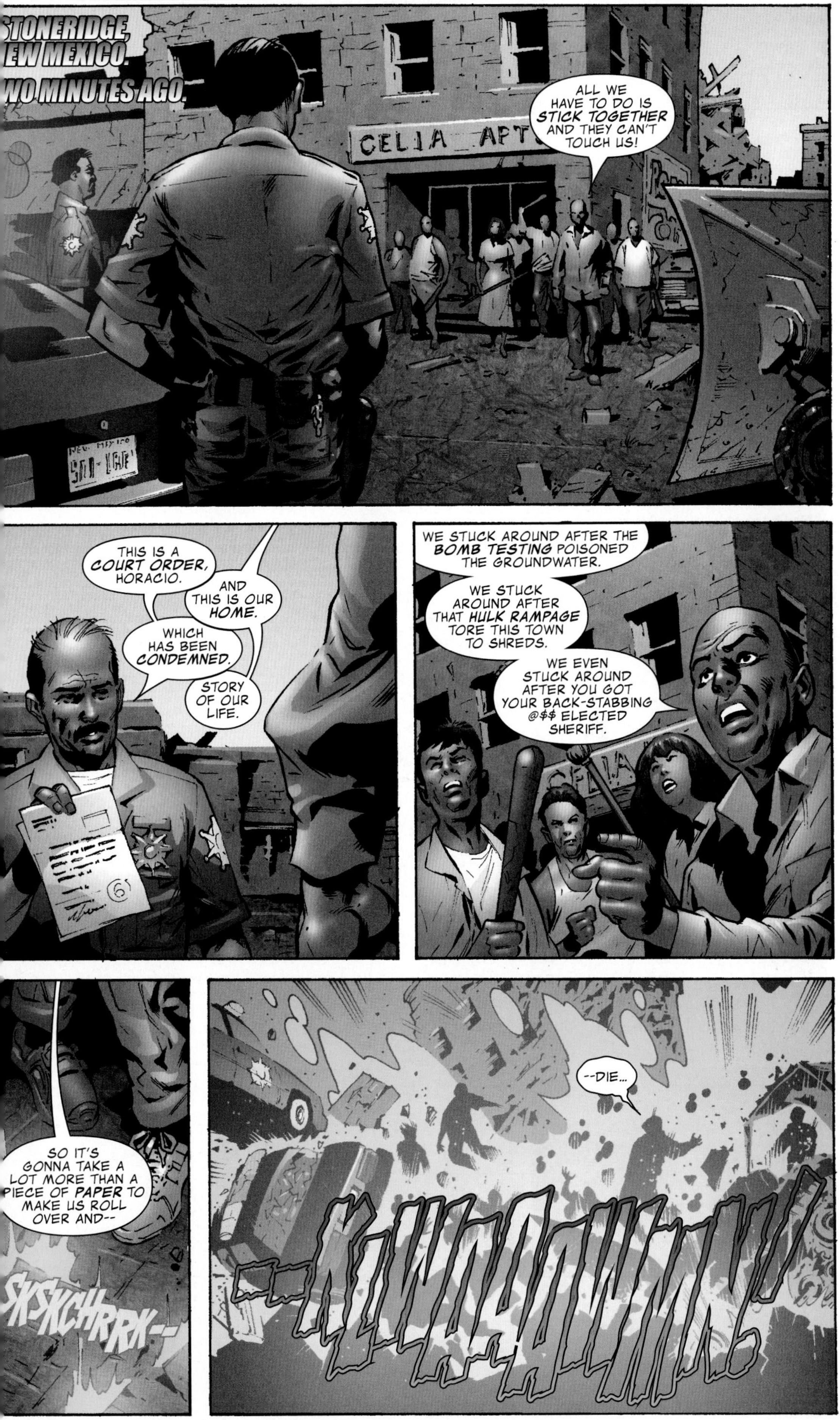

STONERIDGE, NEW MEXICO.
TWO MINUTES AGO.
ALL WE HAVE TO DO IS STICK TOGETHER AND THEY CAN'T TOUCH US!
CELIA APTS
THIS IS A COURT ORDER, HORACIO.
AND THIS IS OUR HOME.
WHICH HAS BEEN CONDEMNED.
STORY OF OUR LIFE.
WE STUCK AROUND AFTER THE BOMB TESTING POISONED THE GROUNDWATER.
WE STUCK AROUND AFTER THAT HULK RAMPAGE TORE THIS TOWN TO SHREDS.
WE EVEN STUCK AROUND AFTER YOU GOT YOUR BACK-STABBING @$$ ELECTED SHERIFF.
SO IT'S GONNA TAKE A LOT MORE THAN A PIECE OF PAPER TO MAKE US ROLL OVER AND--
SKSKCHRRK--
--DIE...

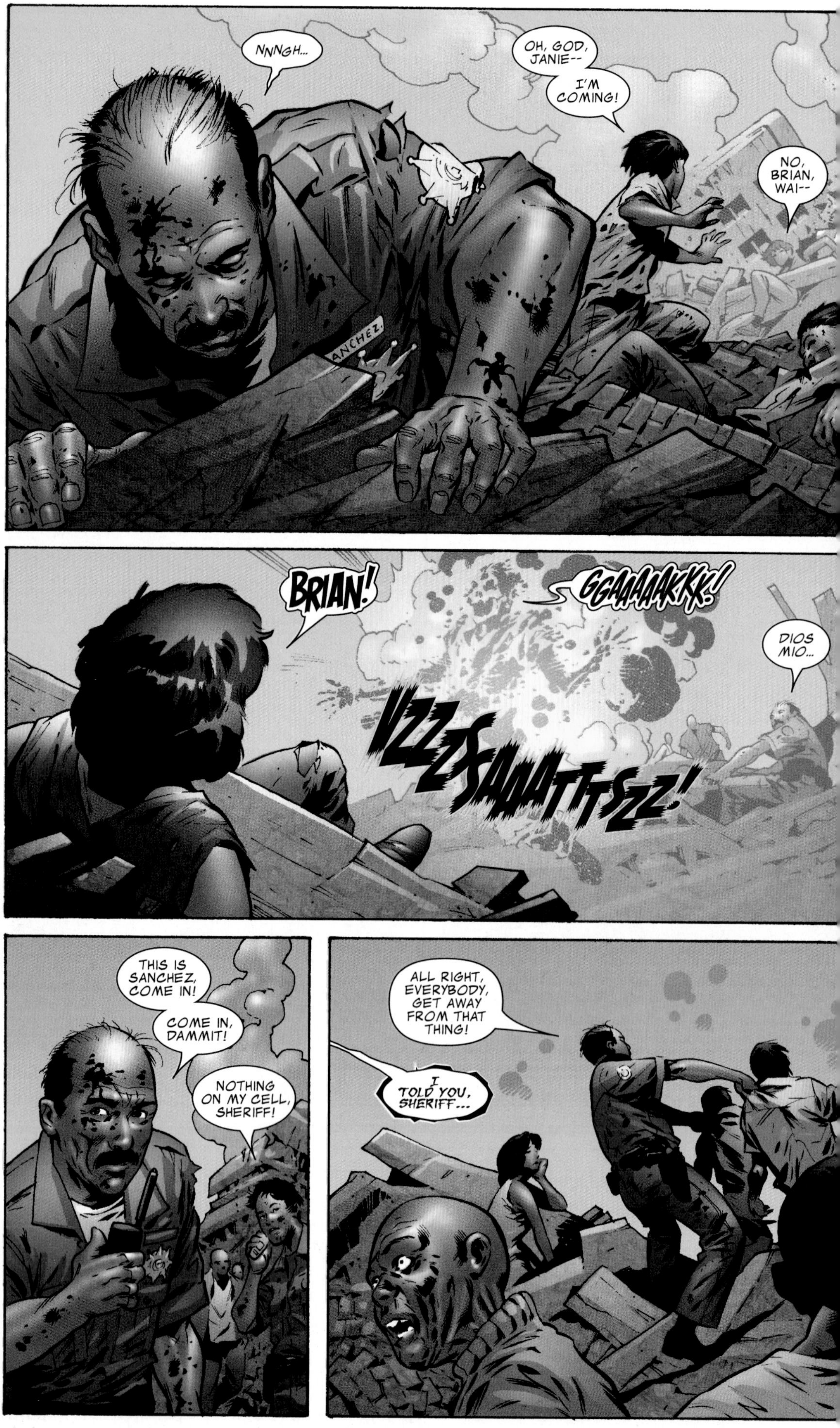
NNNGH...
OH, GOD, JANIE--
I'M COMING!
NO, BRIAN, WAI--
ANCHEZ
BRIAN!
GGAAAAAKKK!
DIOS MIO...
VZZZSAAAATTTSZZ!
THIS IS SANCHEZ, COME IN!
COME IN, DAMMIT!
NOTHING ON MY CELL, SHERIFF!
ALL RIGHT, EVERYBODY, GET AWAY FROM THAT THING!
I TOLD YOU, SHERIFF...

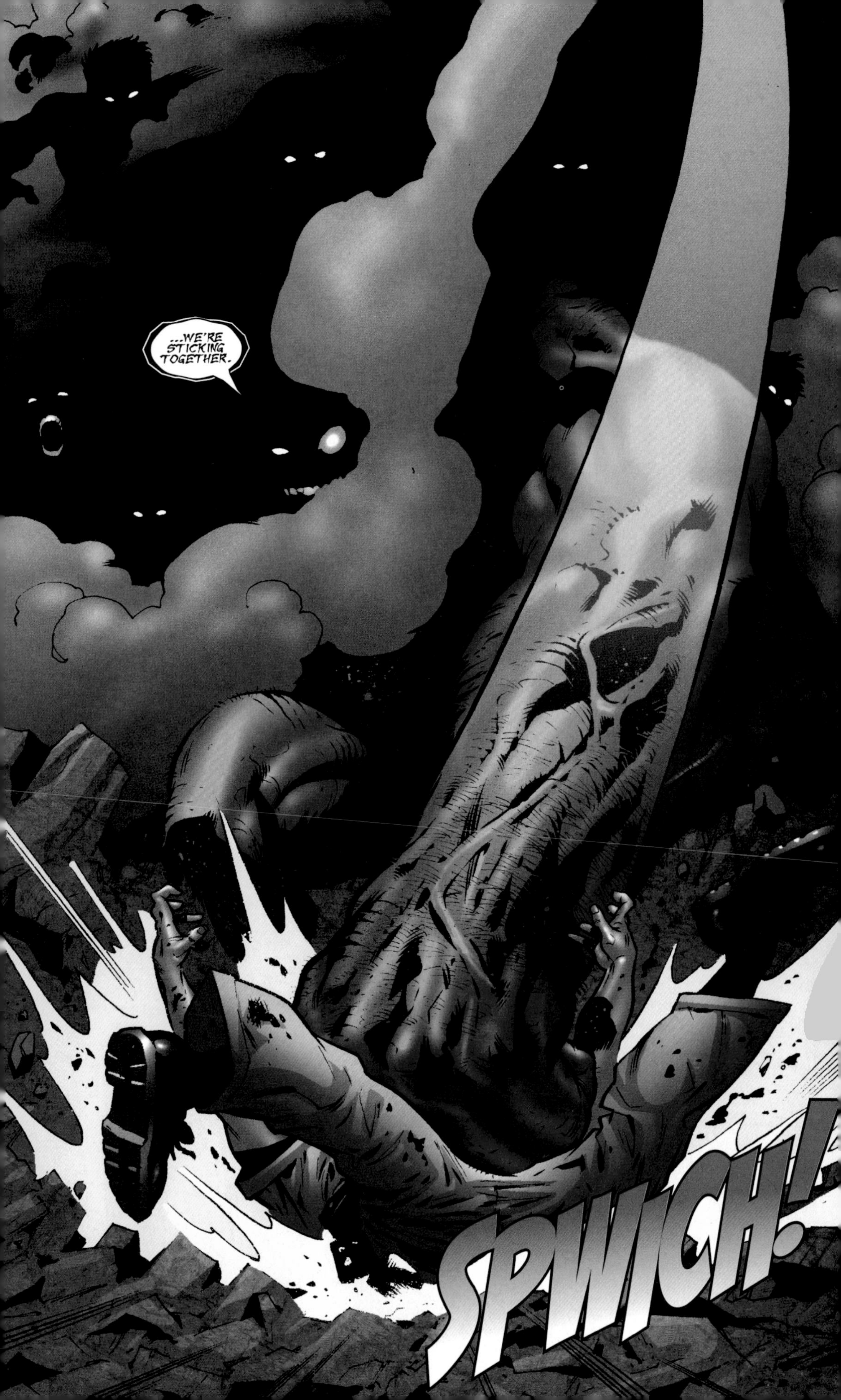
...WE'RE STICKING TOGETHER.
SPWICH!!

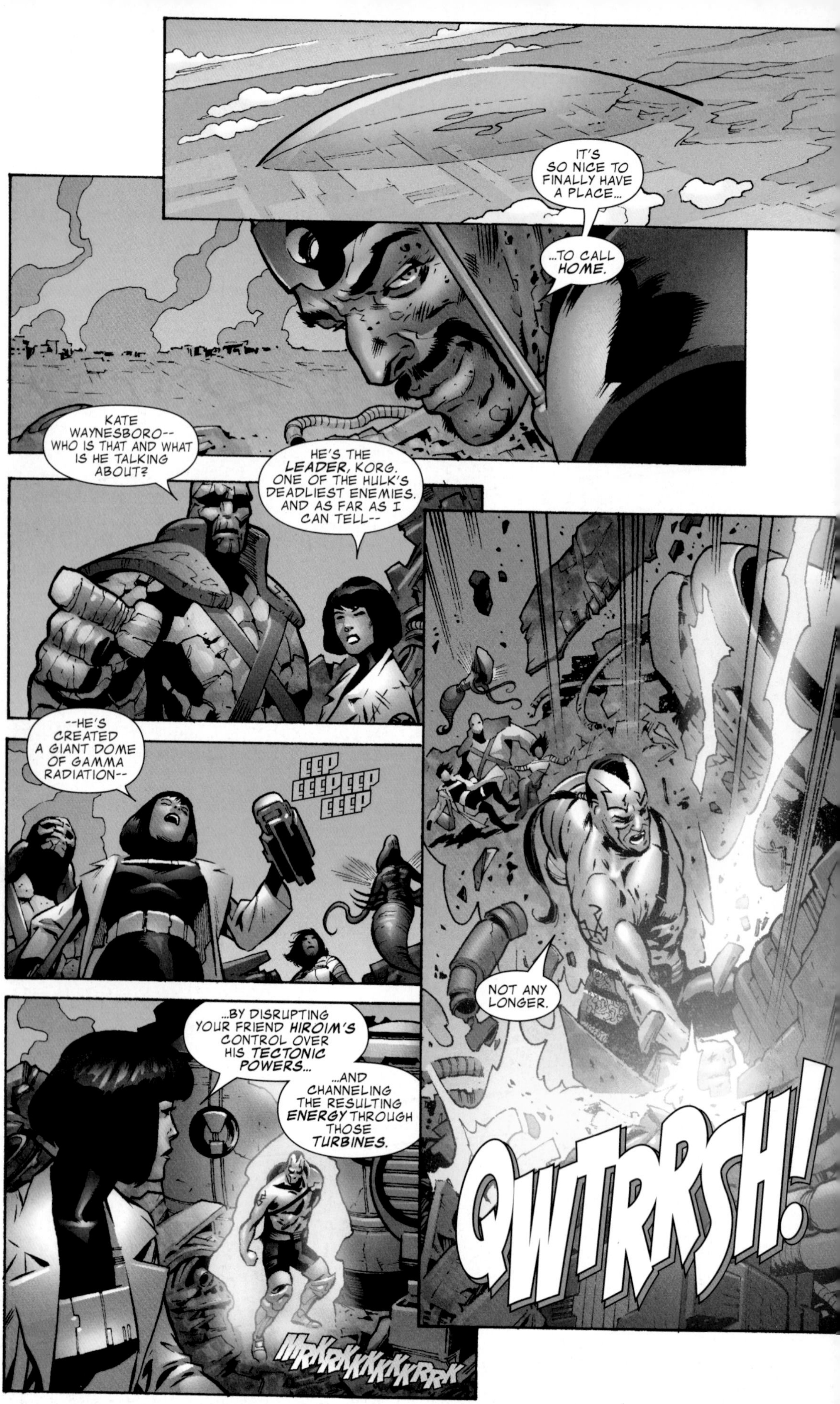
IT'S SO NICE TO FINALLY HAVE A PLACE...
...TO CALL HOME.
KATE WAYNESBORO-- WHO IS THAT AND WHAT IS HE TALKING ABOUT?
HE'S THE LEADER, KORG. ONE OF THE HULK'S DEADLIEST ENEMIES. AND AS FAR AS I CAN TELL--
--HE'S CREATED A GIANT DOME OF GAMMA RADIATION--
EEEP EEEPEEEP EEEP
...BY DISRUPTING YOUR FRIEND HIROIM'S CONTROL OVER HIS TECTONIC POWERS...
...AND CHANNELING THE RESULTING ENERGY THROUGH THOSE TURBINES.
MRKRKKKKKKKRRRK
NOT ANY LONGER.
QWTRRSH!

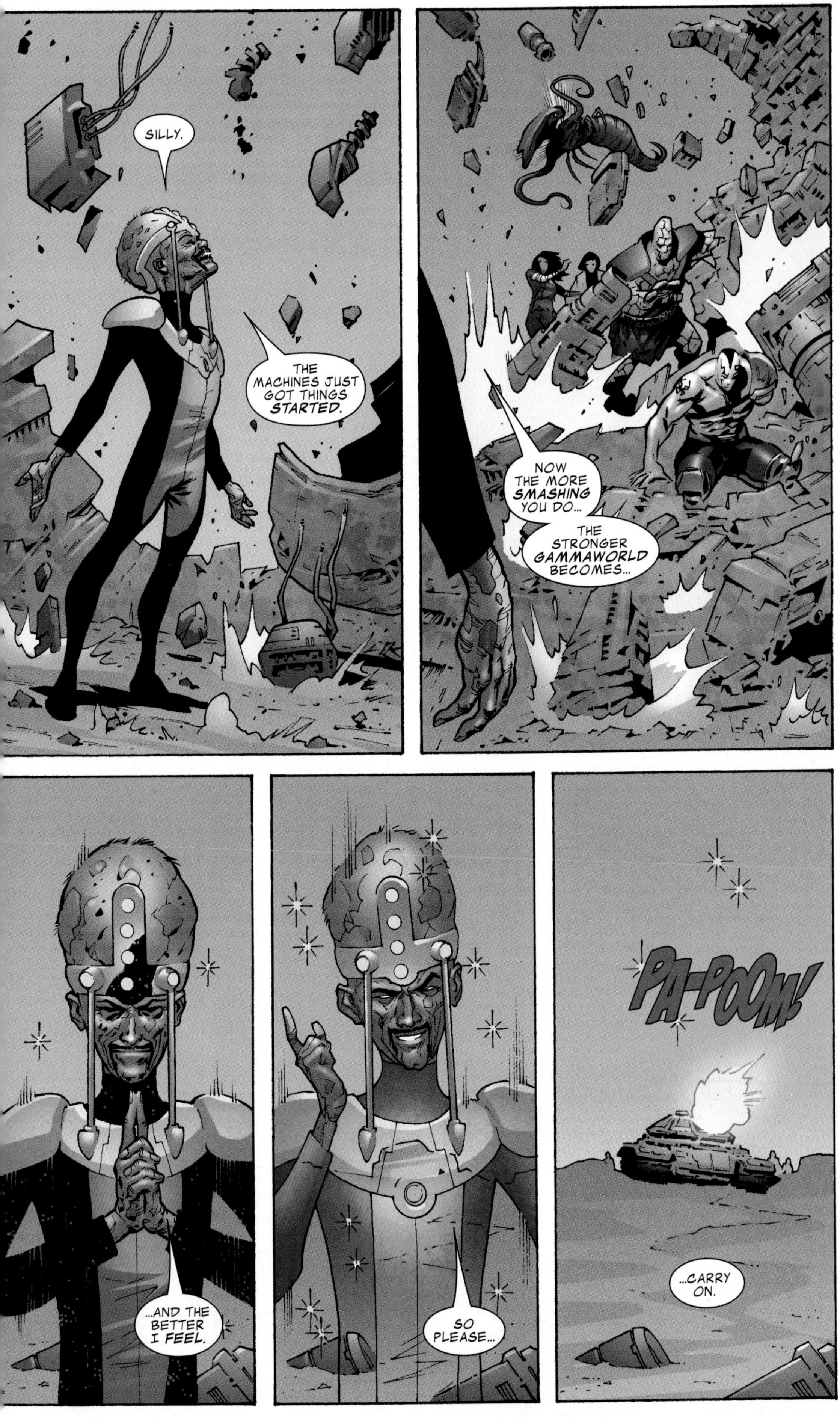
SILLY.
THE MACHINES JUST GOT THINGS STARTED.
NOW THE MORE SMASHING YOU DO...
THE STRONGER GAMMAWORLD BECOMES...
...AND THE BETTER I FEEL.
SO PLEASE...
PA-POOM!
...CARRY ON.

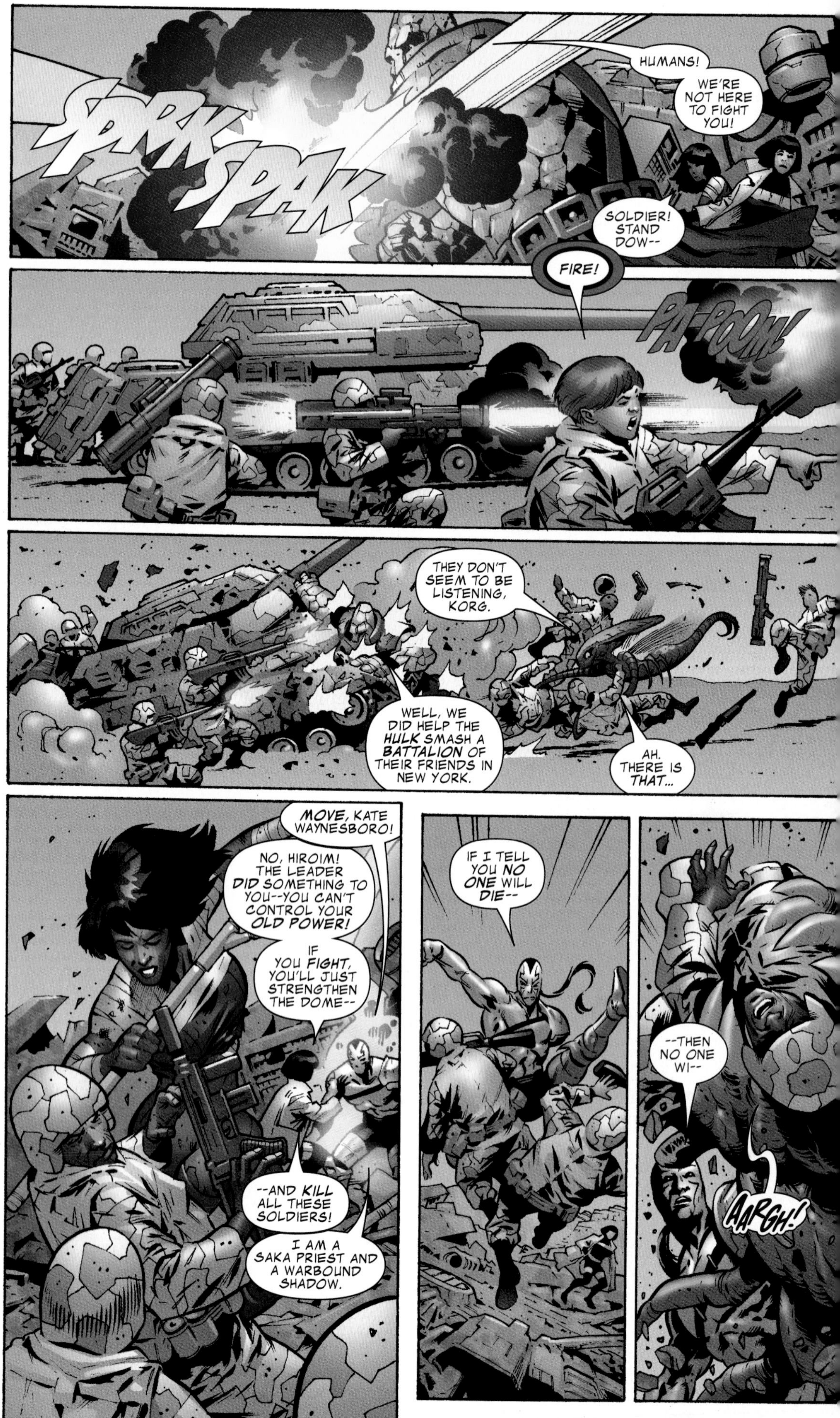
SPAK SPAK
HUMANS!
WE'RE NOT HERE TO FIGHT YOU!
SOLDIER! STAND DOW--
FIRE!
PA-POOM!
THEY DON'T SEEM TO BE LISTENING, KORG.
WELL, WE DID HELP THE HULK SMASH A BATTALION OF THEIR FRIENDS IN NEW YORK.
AH. THERE IS THAT...
MOVE, KATE WAYNESBORO!
NO, HIROIM! THE LEADER DID SOMETHING TO YOU--YOU CAN'T CONTROL YOUR OLD POWER!
IF YOU FIGHT, YOU'LL JUST STRENGTHEN THE DOME--
--AND KILL ALL THESE SOLDIERS!
I AM A SAKA PRIEST AND A WARBOUND SHADOW.
IF I TELL YOU NO ONE WILL DIE--
--THEN NO ONE WI--
AARGH!

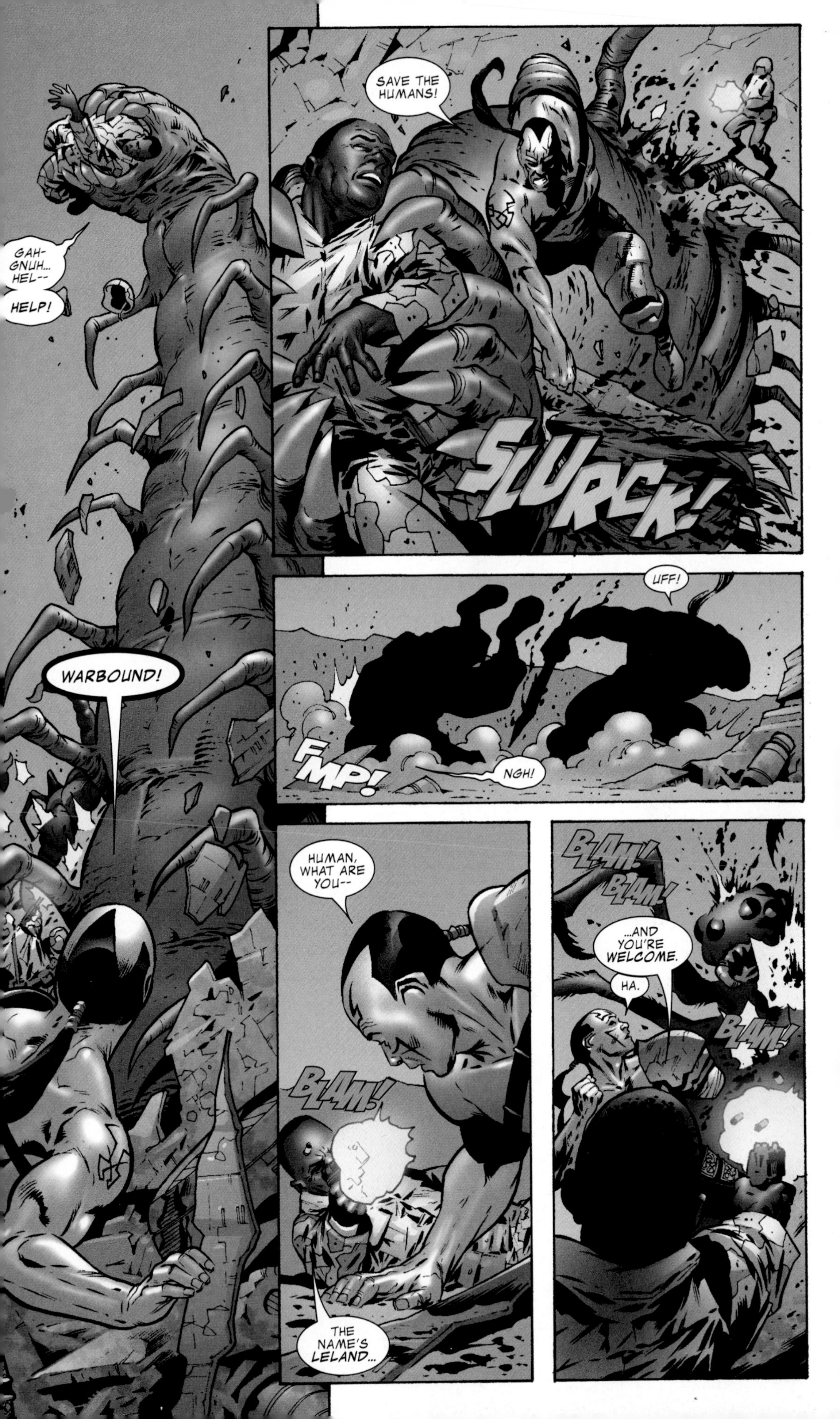
GAH-GNUH... HEL--
HELP!
SAVE THE HUMANS!
SLURCK!
WARBOUND!
UFF!
FMP!
NGH!
HUMAN, WHAT ARE YOU--
BLAM!
THE NAME'S LELAND...
BLAM! BLAM!
...AND YOU'RE WELCOME.
HA.
BLAM!

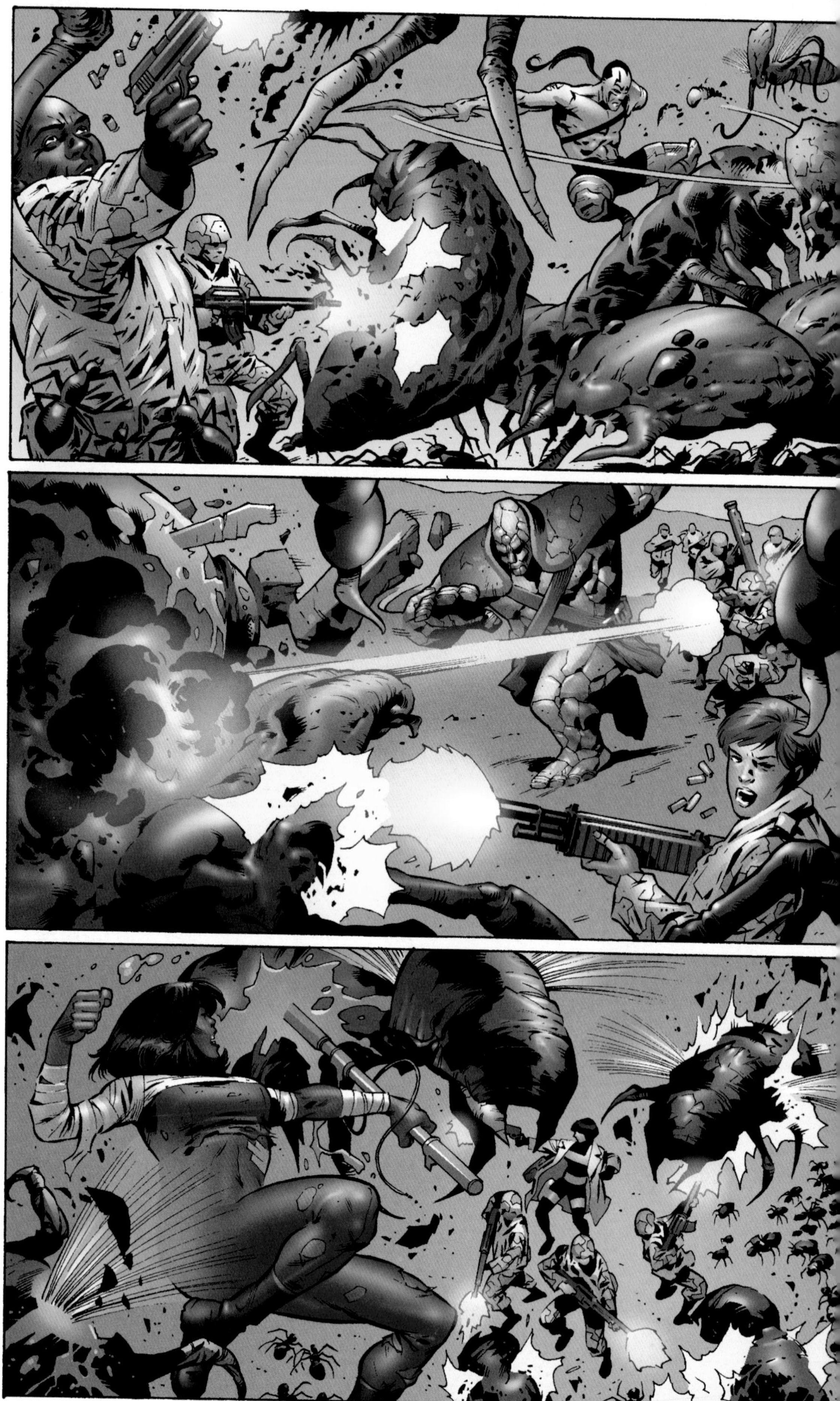

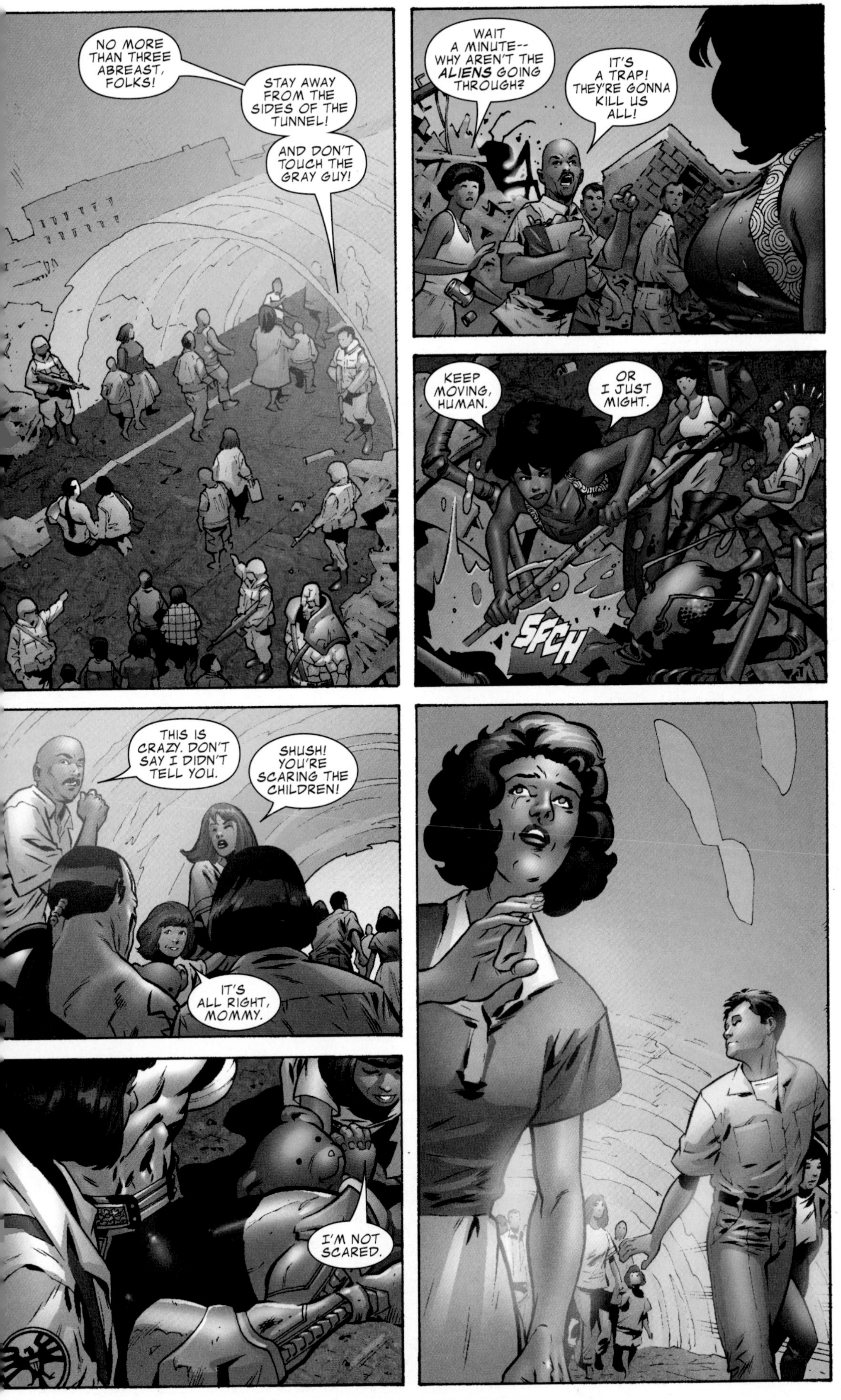
NO MORE THAN THREE ABREAST, FOLKS!
STAY AWAY FROM THE SIDES OF THE TUNNEL!
AND DON'T TOUCH THE GRAY GUY!
WAIT A MINUTE-- WHY AREN'T THE **ALIENS** GOING THROUGH?
IT'S A TRAP! THEY'RE GONNA KILL US ALL!
KEEP MOVING, HUMAN.
OR I JUST MIGHT.
SFCH
THIS IS CRAZY. DON'T SAY I DIDN'T TELL YOU.
SHUSH! YOU'RE SCARING THE CHILDREN!
IT'S ALL RIGHT, MOMMY.
I'M NOT SCARED.

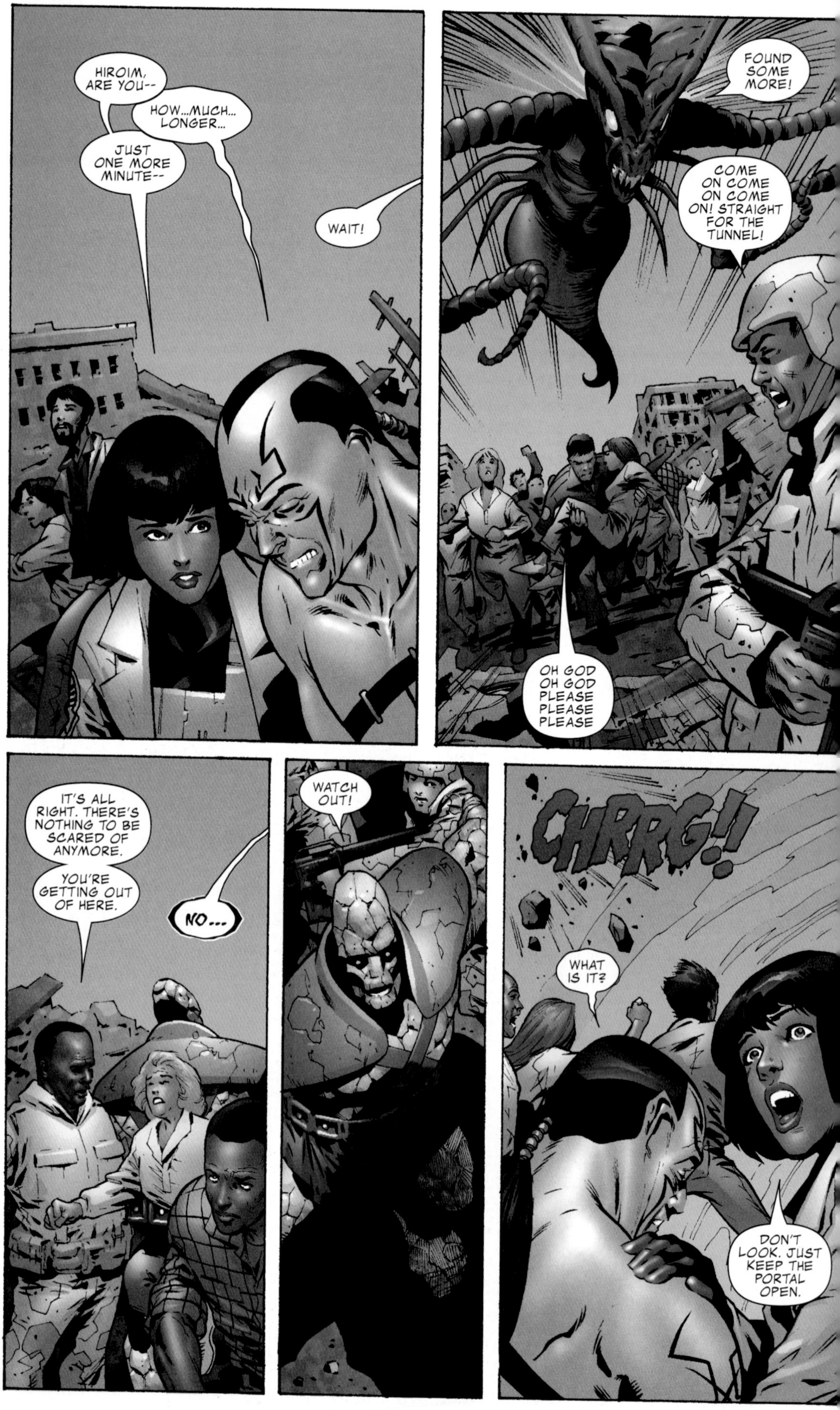
HIROIM, ARE YOU--
HOW...MUCH... LONGER...
JUST ONE MORE MINUTE--
WAIT!
FOUND SOME MORE!
COME ON COME ON COME ON! STRAIGHT FOR THE TUNNEL!
OH GOD OH GOD PLEASE PLEASE PLEASE
IT'S ALL RIGHT. THERE'S NOTHING TO BE SCARED OF ANYMORE.
YOU'RE GETTING OUT OF HERE.
NO...
WATCH OUT!
CHRRG!!
WHAT IS IT?
DON'T LOOK. JUST KEEP THE PORTAL OPEN.

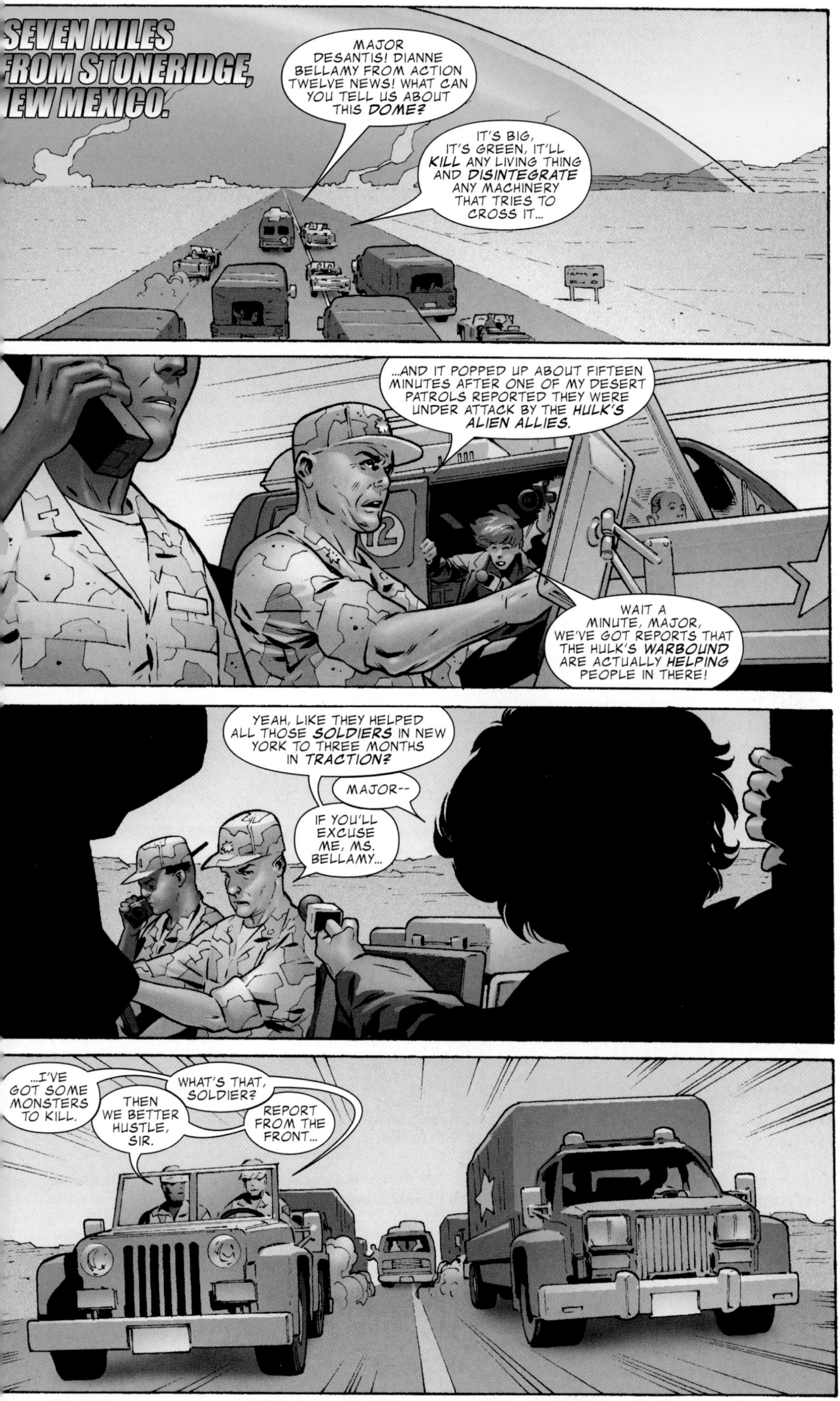
SEVEN MILES FROM STONERIDGE, NEW MEXICO.
MAJOR DESANTIS! DIANNE BELLAMY FROM ACTION TWELVE NEWS! WHAT CAN YOU TELL US ABOUT THIS DOME?
IT'S BIG, IT'S GREEN, IT'LL KILL ANY LIVING THING AND DISINTEGRATE ANY MACHINERY THAT TRIES TO CROSS IT...
...AND IT POPPED UP ABOUT FIFTEEN MINUTES AFTER ONE OF MY DESERT PATROLS REPORTED THEY WERE UNDER ATTACK BY THE HULK'S ALIEN ALLIES.
12
WAIT A MINUTE, MAJOR, WE'VE GOT REPORTS THAT THE HULK'S WARBOUND ARE ACTUALLY HELPING PEOPLE IN THERE!
YEAH, LIKE THEY HELPED ALL THOSE SOLDIERS IN NEW YORK TO THREE MONTHS IN TRACTION?
MAJOR--
IF YOU'LL EXCUSE ME, MS. BELLAMY...
...I'VE GOT SOME MONSTERS TO KILL.
WHAT'S THAT, SOLDIER?
REPORT FROM THE FRONT...
THEN WE BETTER HUSTLE, SIR.

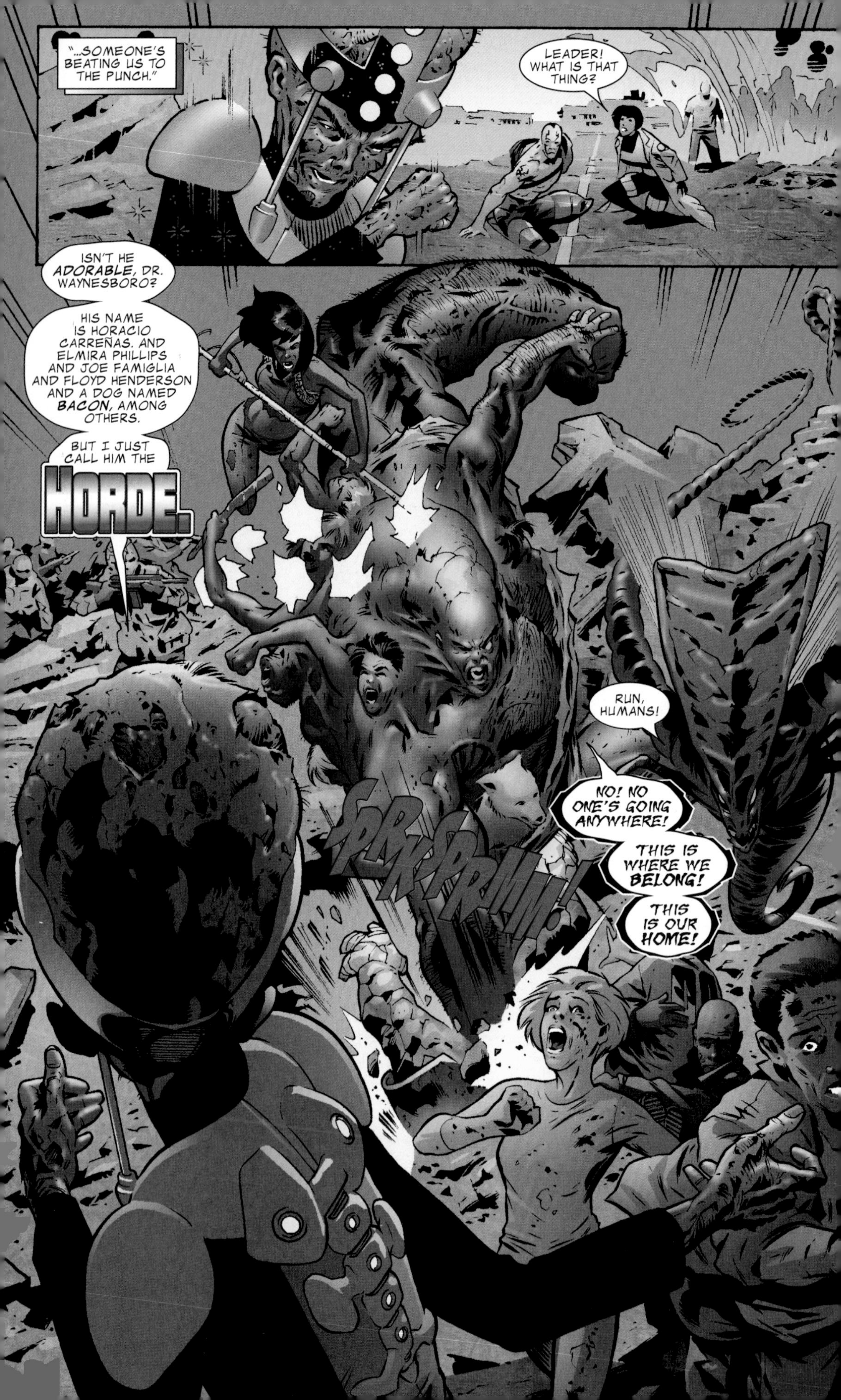
"...SOMEONE'S BEATING US TO THE PUNCH."
LEADER! WHAT IS THAT THING?
ISN'T HE *ADORABLE*, DR. WAYNESBORO?
HIS NAME IS HORACIO CARREÑAS. AND ELMIRA PHILLIPS AND JOE FAMIGLIA AND FLOYD HENDERSON AND A DOG NAMED *BACON*, AMONG OTHERS.
BUT I JUST CALL HIM THE
HORDE.
RUN, HUMANS!
SPRK SPRMM!
NO! NO ONE'S GOING ANYWHERE!
THIS IS WHERE WE *BELONG!*
THIS IS OUR *HOME!*

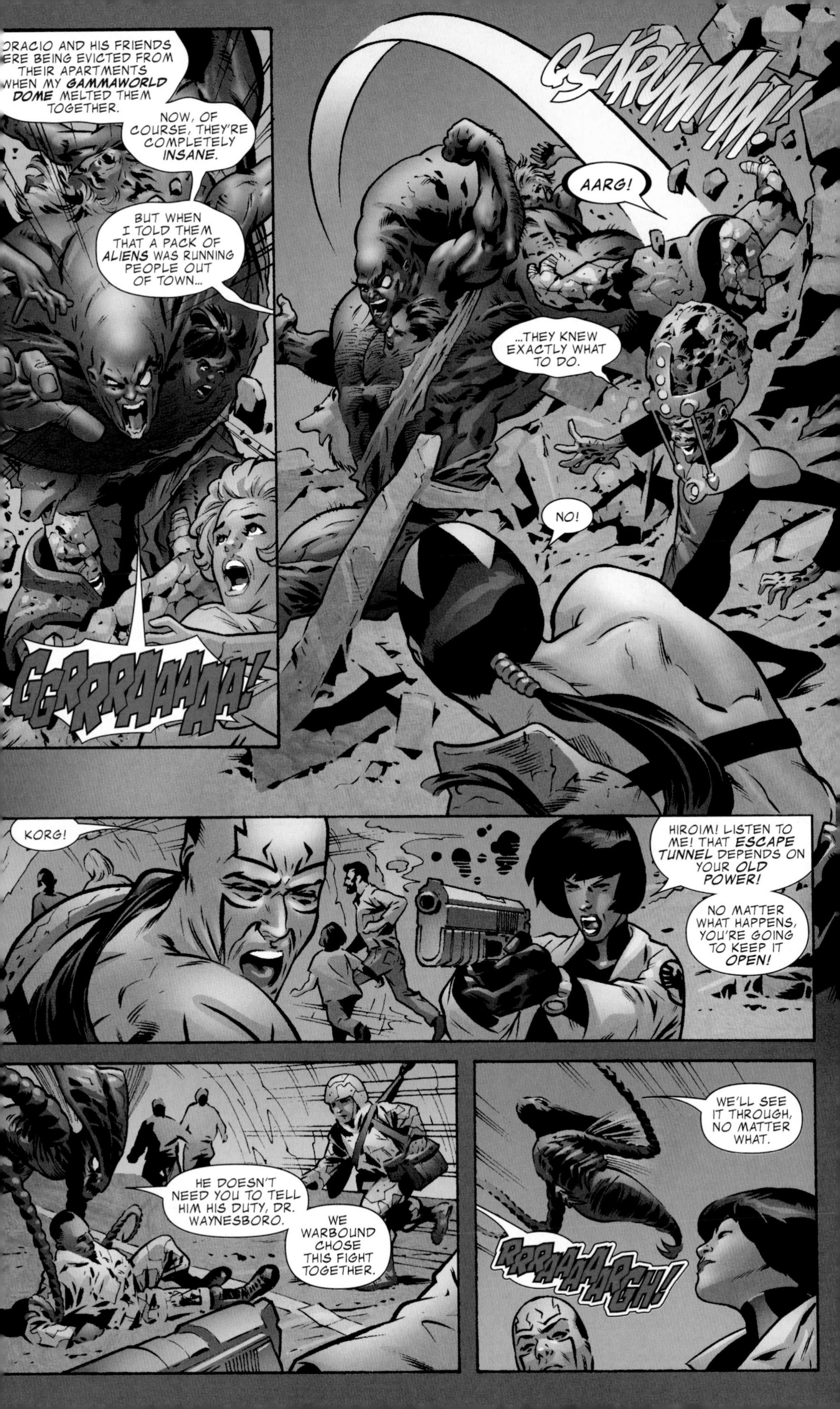

ORACIO AND HIS FRIENDS ERE BEING EVICTED FROM THEIR APARTMENTS WHEN MY GAMMAWORLD DOME MELTED THEM TOGETHER.
NOW, OF COURSE, THEY'RE COMPLETELY INSANE.
BUT WHEN I TOLD THEM THAT A PACK OF ALIENS WAS RUNNING PEOPLE OUT OF TOWN...
GGRRRAAAAAA!
KRUMMM!
AARG!
...THEY KNEW EXACTLY WHAT TO DO.
NO!
KORG!
HIROIM! LISTEN TO ME! THAT ESCAPE TUNNEL DEPENDS ON YOUR OLD POWER!
NO MATTER WHAT HAPPENS, YOU'RE GOING TO KEEP IT OPEN!
HE DOESN'T NEED YOU TO TELL HIM HIS DUTY, DR. WAYNESBORO.
WE WARBOUND CHOSE THIS FIGHT TOGETHER.
WE'LL SEE IT THROUGH, NO MATTER WHAT.
RRRAAAAARGH!

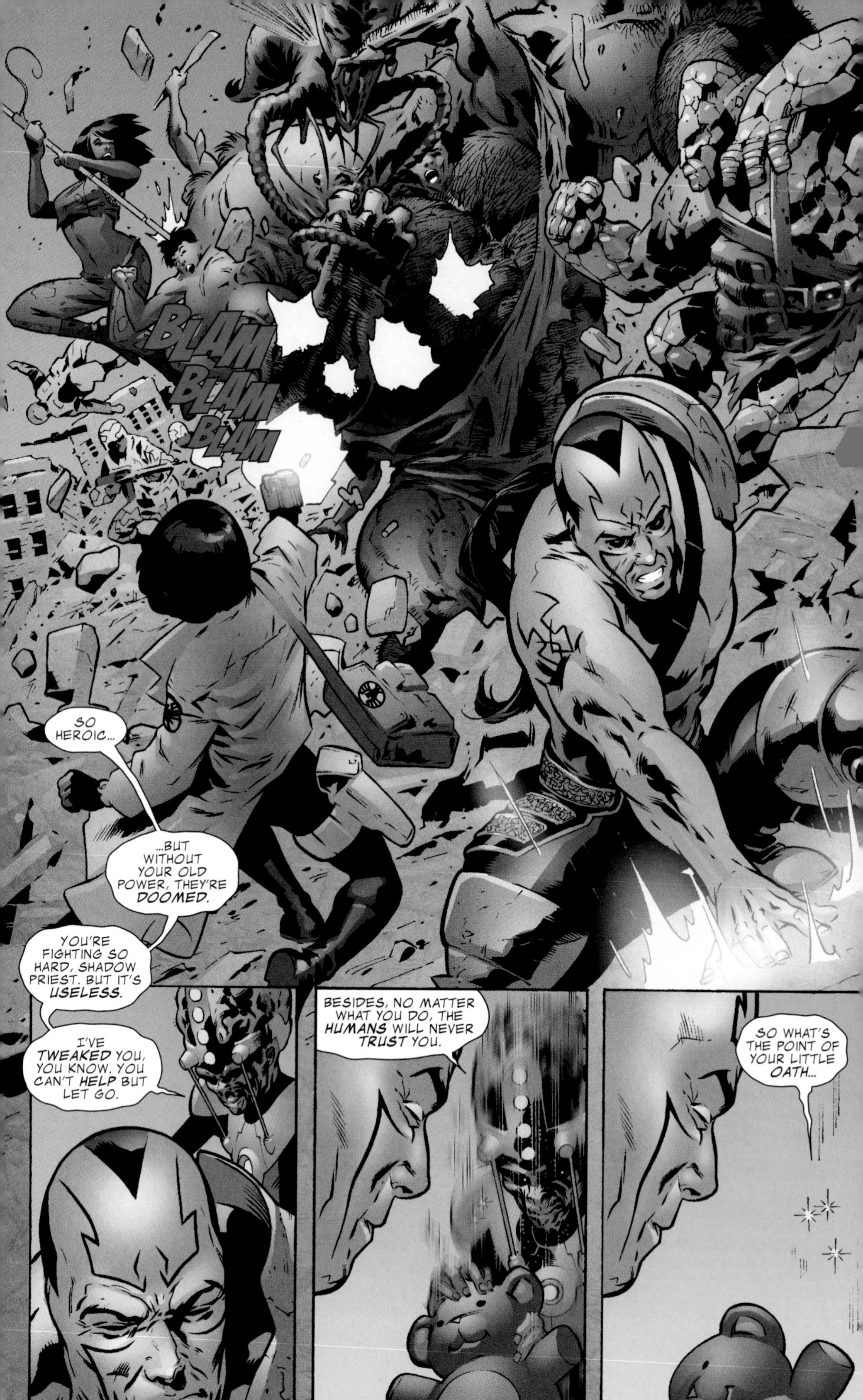
BLAM BLAM BLAM
SO HEROIC...
...BUT WITHOUT YOUR OLD POWER, THEY'RE *DOOMED*.
YOU'RE FIGHTING SO HARD, SHADOW PRIEST. BUT IT'S *USELESS*.
I'VE *TWEAKED* YOU, YOU KNOW. YOU CAN'T *HELP* BUT LET GO.
BESIDES, NO MATTER WHAT YOU DO, THE *HUMANS* WILL NEVER *TRUST* YOU.
SO WHAT'S THE POINT OF YOUR LITTLE *OATH*...

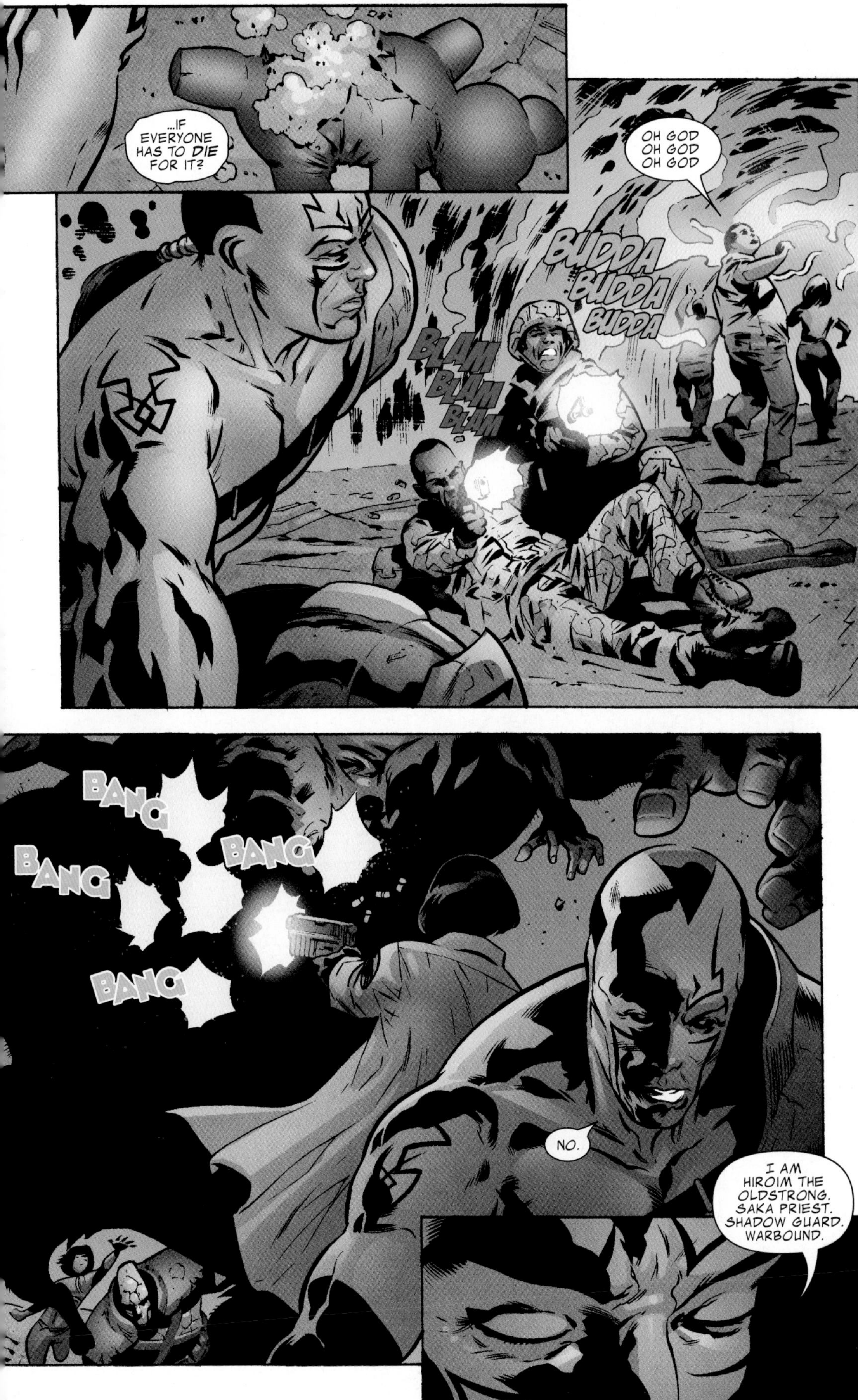
...IF EVERYONE HAS TO DIE FOR IT?
OH GOD OH GOD OH GOD
BUDDA BUDDA BUDDA
BLAM BLAM BLAM
BANG
BANG
BANG
BANG
NO.
I AM HIROIM THE OLDSTRONG. SAKA PRIEST. SHADOW GUARD. WARBOUND.

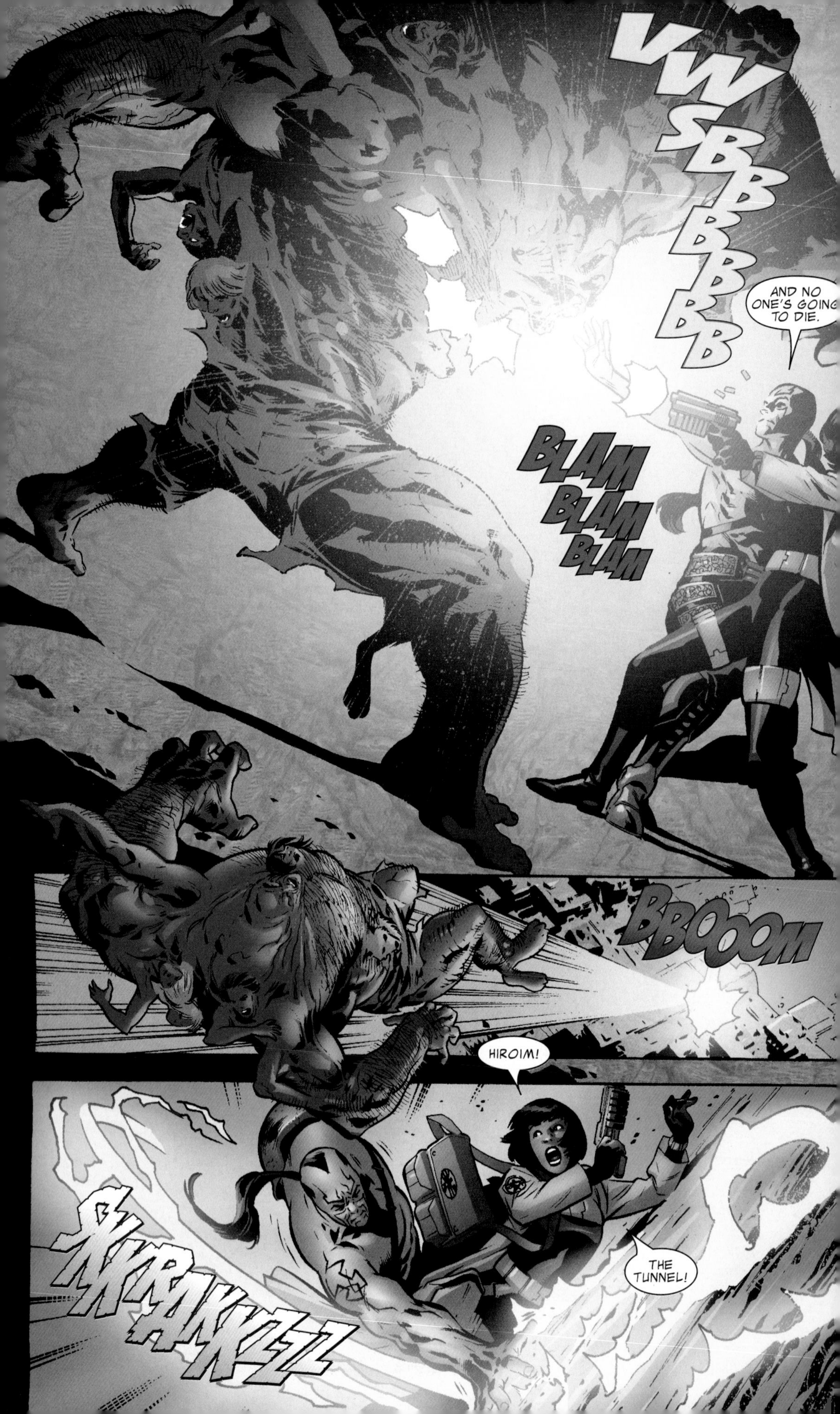
VWSBBBBBB
AND NO ONE'S GOING TO DIE.
BLAM BLAM BLAM
BBOOOM
HIROIM!
SKRAKKZZZ
THE TUNNEL!

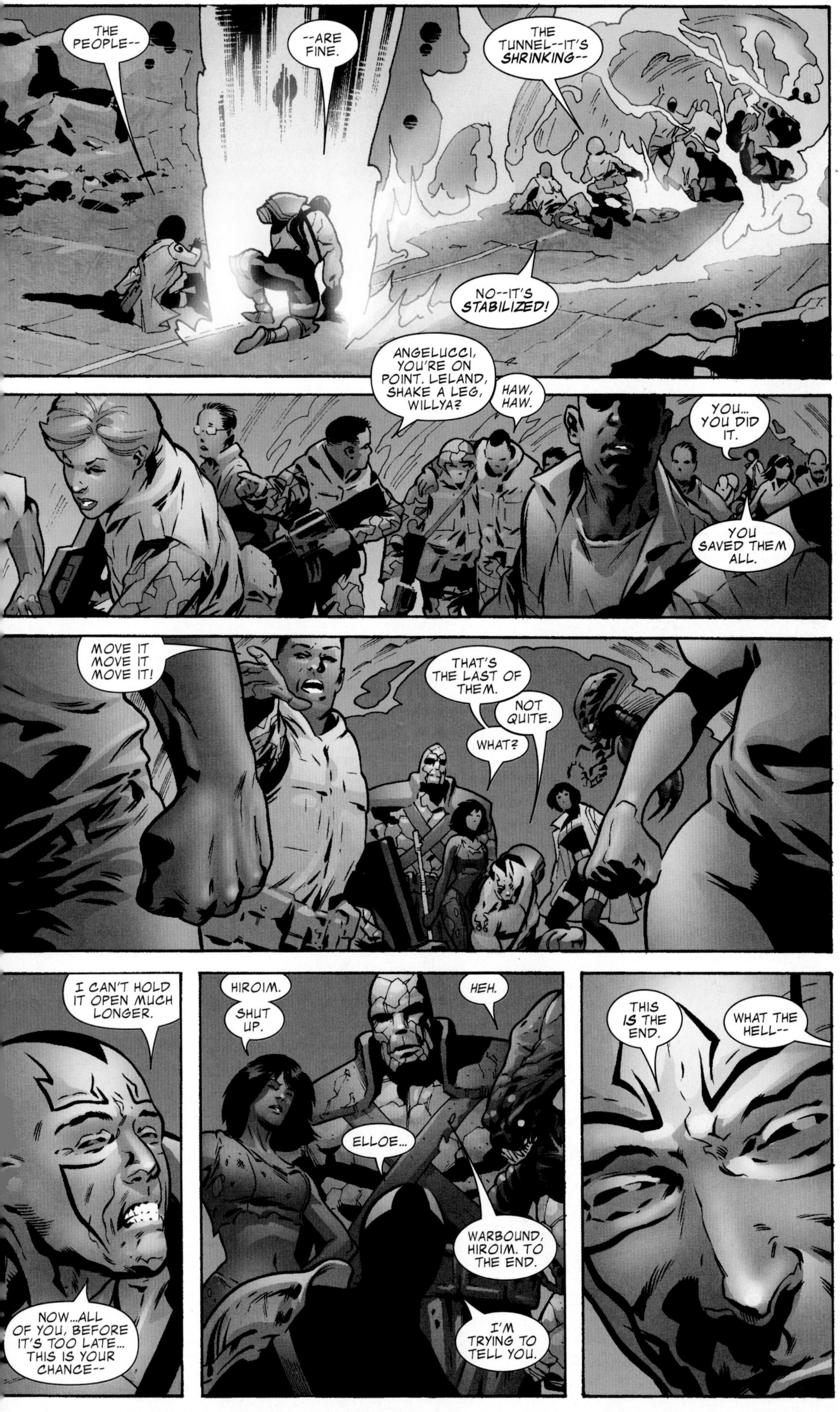
THE PEOPLE--
--ARE FINE.
THE TUNNEL--IT'S SHRINKING--
NO--IT'S STABILIZED!
ANGELUCCI, YOU'RE ON POINT. LELAND, SHAKE A LEG, WILLYA?
HAW, HAW.
YOU... YOU DID IT.
YOU SAVED THEM ALL.
MOVE IT MOVE IT MOVE IT!
THAT'S THE LAST OF THEM.
NOT QUITE.
WHAT?
I CAN'T HOLD IT OPEN MUCH LONGER.
NOW...ALL OF YOU, BEFORE IT'S TOO LATE... THIS IS YOUR CHANCE--
HIROIM.
SHUT UP.
HEH.
ELLOE...
WARBOUND, HIROIM. TO THE END.
I'M TRYING TO TELL YOU.
THIS IS THE END.
WHAT THE HELL--

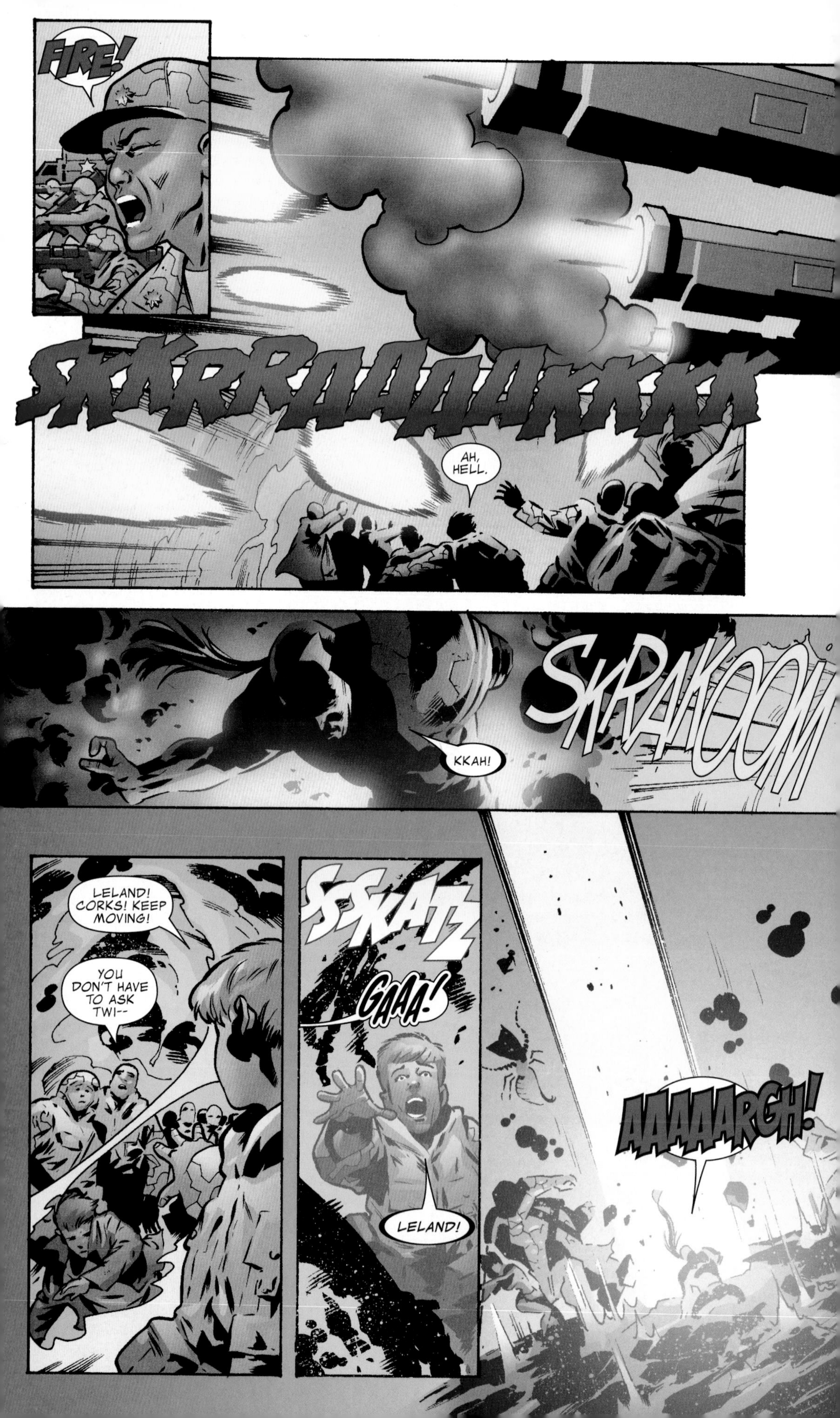
FIRE!
SKRROOOOKKKK
AH, HELL.
KKAH!
SKRAKOOM
LELAND! CORKS! KEEP MOVING!
YOU DON'T HAVE TO ASK TWI--
SSKATZ
GAAA!
LELAND!
AAAAARGH!

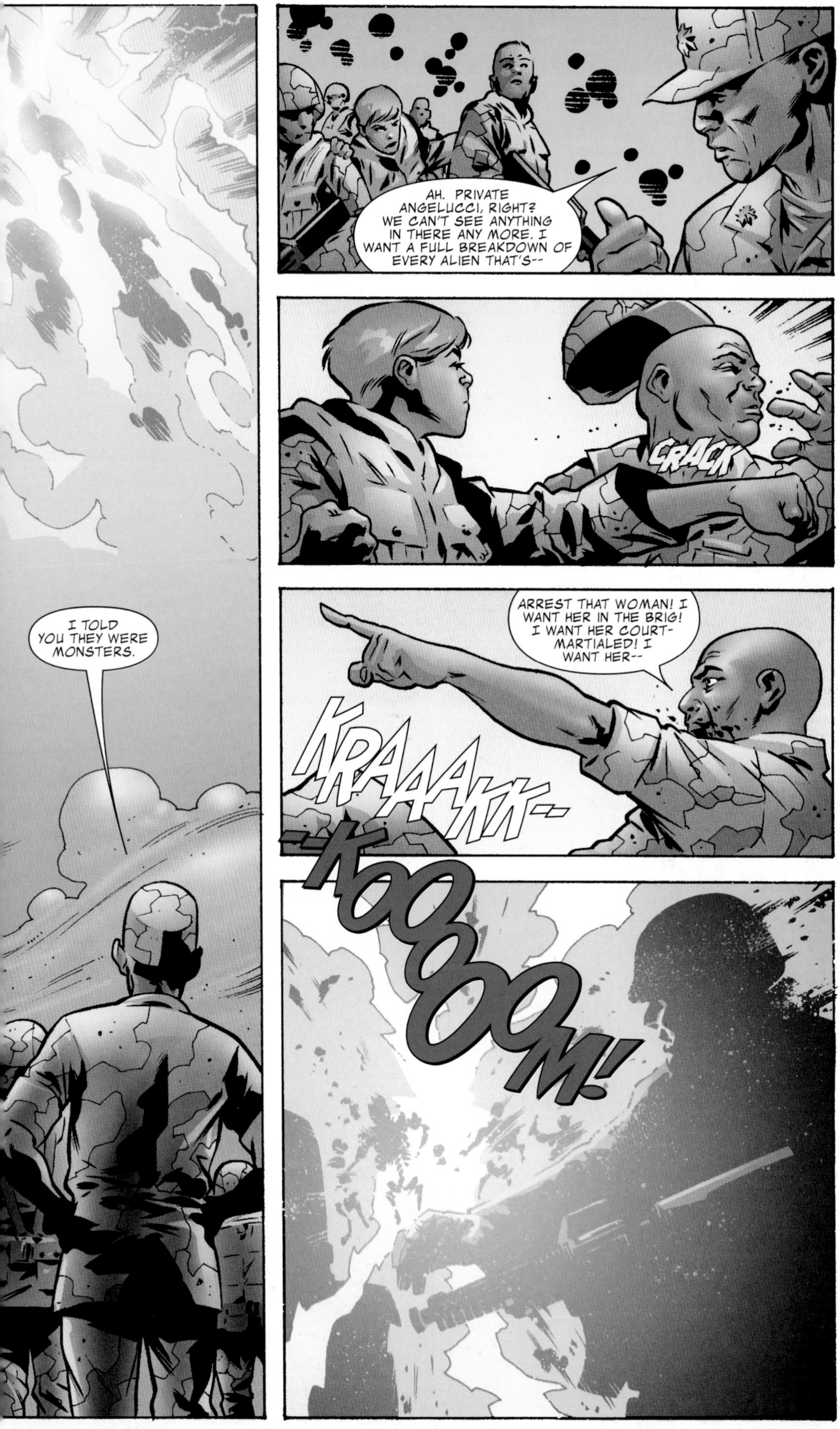
AH. PRIVATE ANGELUCCI, RIGHT? WE CAN'T SEE ANYTHING IN THERE ANY MORE. I WANT A FULL BREAKDOWN OF EVERY ALIEN THAT'S--
CRACK
ARREST THAT WOMAN! I WANT HER IN THE BRIG! I WANT HER COURT-MARTIALED! I WANT HER--
KRAAAKK--
--KOOOOOM!
I TOLD YOU THEY WERE MONSTERS.

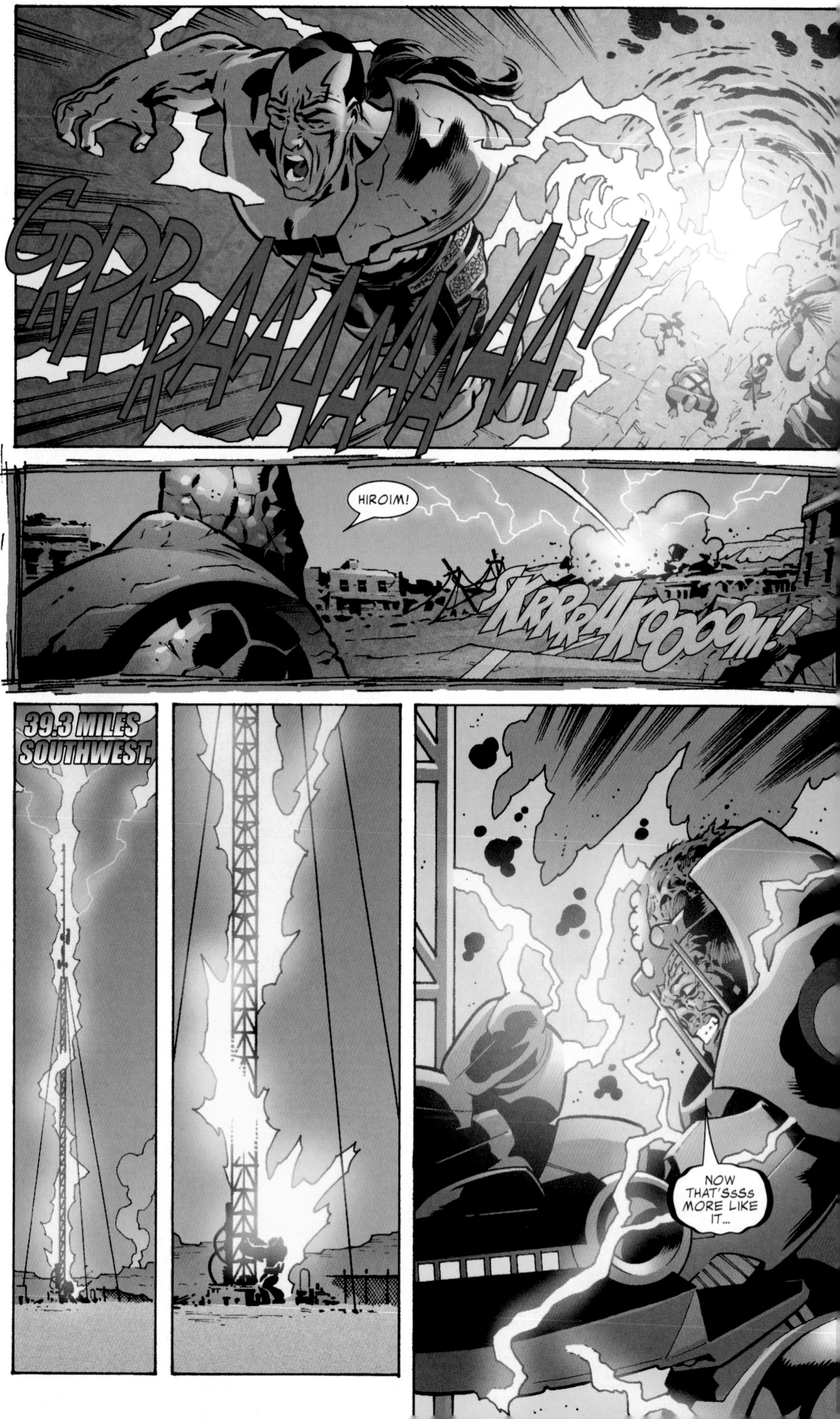

GRRRAAAAAAAA!
HIROIM!
KRRRAKOOOOM!
39.3 MILES SOUTHWEST.
NOW THAT'SSSS MORE LIKE IT...

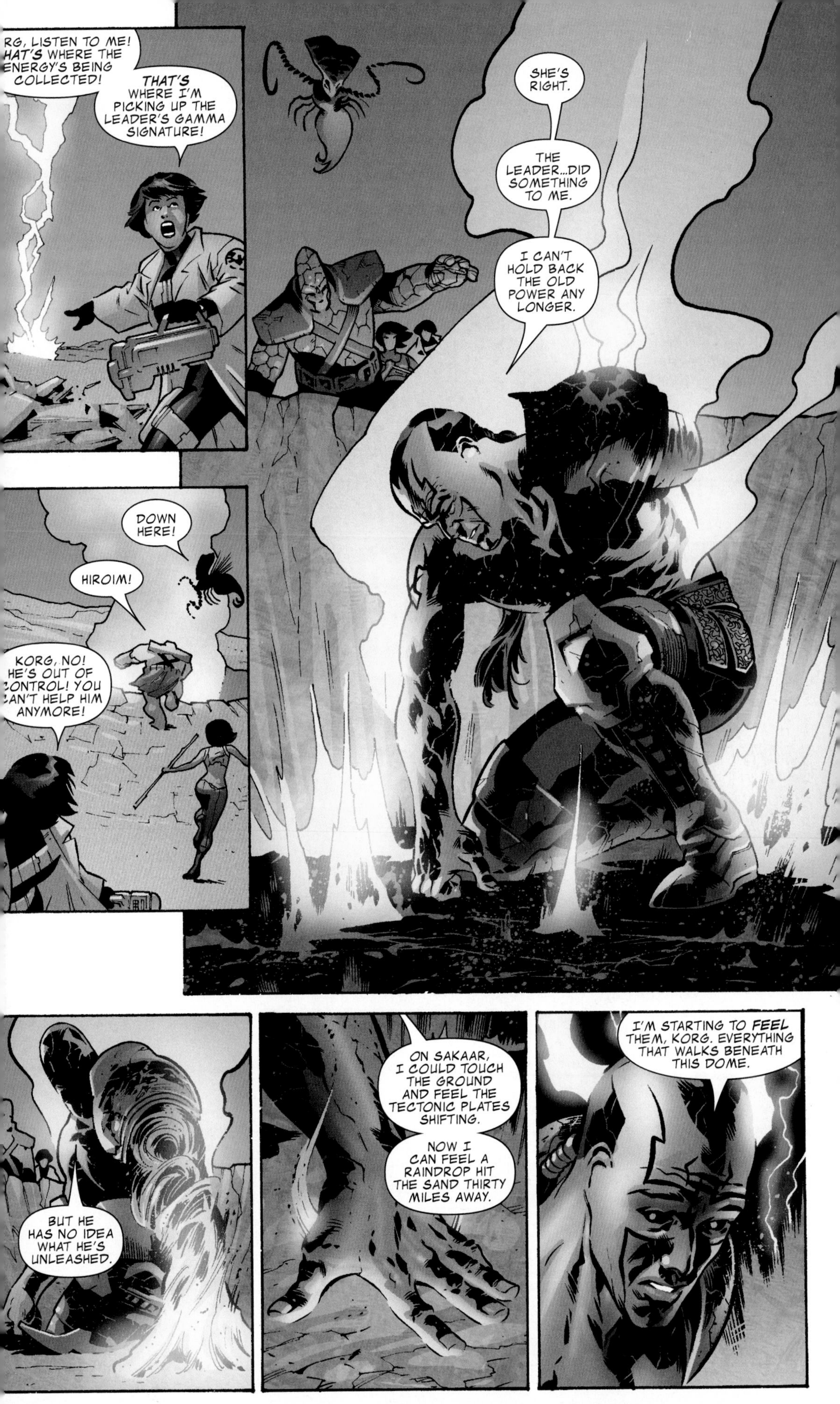

RG, LISTEN TO ME! HAT'S WHERE THE ENERGY'S BEING COLLECTED!
THAT'S WHERE I'M PICKING UP THE LEADER'S GAMMA SIGNATURE!
SHE'S RIGHT.
THE LEADER...DID SOMETHING TO ME.
I CAN'T HOLD BACK THE OLD POWER ANY LONGER.
DOWN HERE!
HIROIM!
KORG, NO! HE'S OUT OF CONTROL! YOU CAN'T HELP HIM ANYMORE!
BUT HE HAS NO IDEA WHAT HE'S UNLEASHED.
ON SAKAAR, I COULD TOUCH THE GROUND AND FEEL THE TECTONIC PLATES SHIFTING.
NOW I CAN FEEL A RAINDROP HIT THE SAND THIRTY MILES AWAY.
I'M STARTING TO FEEL THEM, KORG. EVERYTHING THAT WALKS BENEATH THIS DOME.

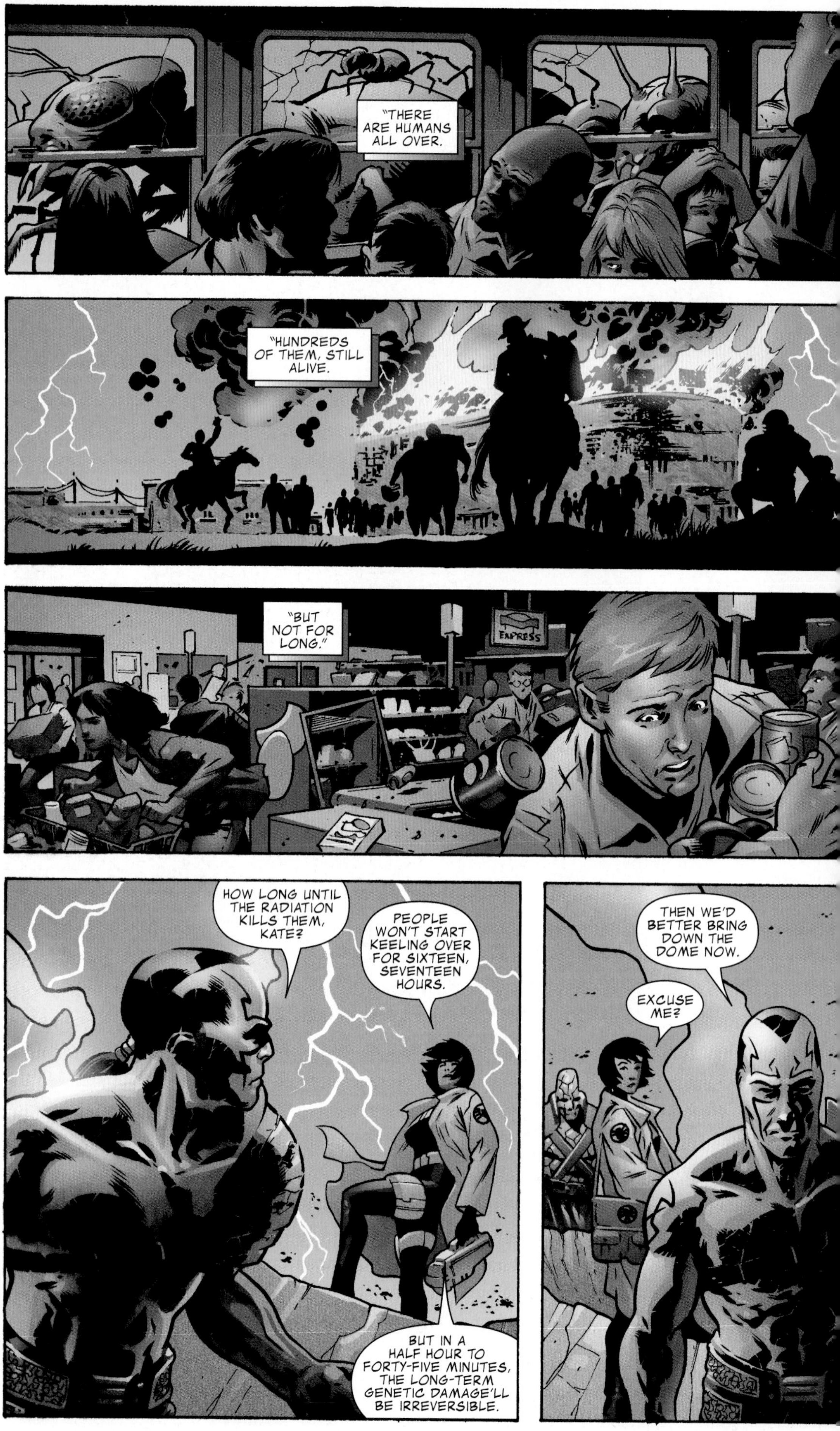
"THERE ARE HUMANS ALL OVER.
"HUNDREDS OF THEM, STILL ALIVE.
"BUT NOT FOR LONG."
EXPRESS
HOW LONG UNTIL THE RADIATION KILLS THEM, KATE?
PEOPLE WON'T START KEELING OVER FOR SIXTEEN, SEVENTEEN HOURS.
BUT IN A HALF HOUR TO FORTY-FIVE MINUTES, THE LONG-TERM GENETIC DAMAGE'LL BE IRREVERSIBLE.
THEN WE'D BETTER BRING DOWN THE DOME NOW.
EXCUSE ME?

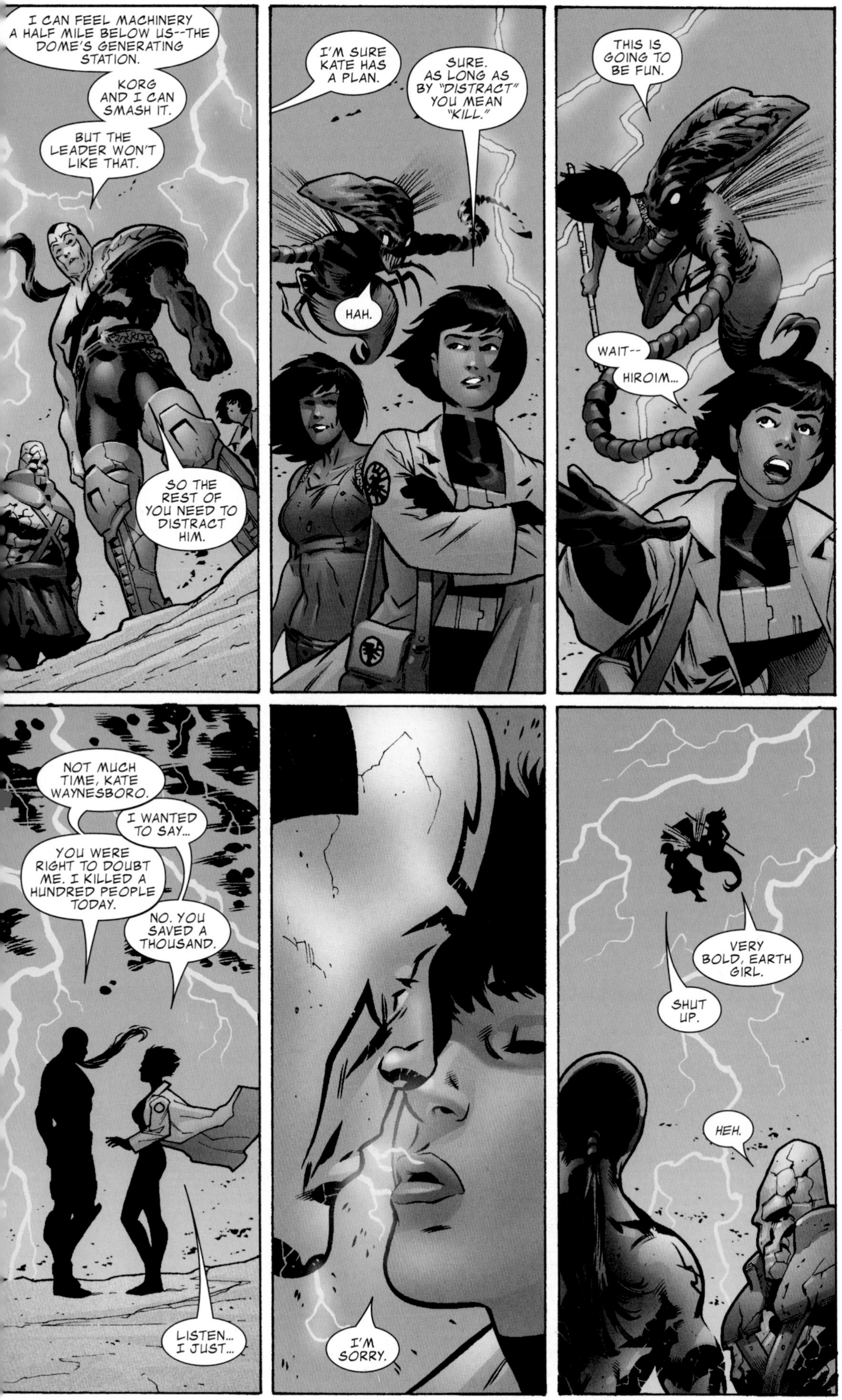
I CAN FEEL MACHINERY A HALF MILE BELOW US--THE DOME'S GENERATING STATION.
KORG AND I CAN SMASH IT.
BUT THE LEADER WON'T LIKE THAT.
SO THE REST OF YOU NEED TO DISTRACT HIM.
I'M SURE KATE HAS A PLAN.
SURE. AS LONG AS BY "DISTRACT" YOU MEAN "KILL."
HAH.
THIS IS GOING TO BE FUN.
WAIT--
HIROIM...
NOT MUCH TIME, KATE WAYNESBORO.
I WANTED TO SAY...
YOU WERE RIGHT TO DOUBT ME. I KILLED A HUNDRED PEOPLE TODAY.
NO. YOU SAVED A THOUSAND.
LISTEN... I JUST...
I'M SORRY.
VERY BOLD, EARTH GIRL.
SHUT UP.
HEH.

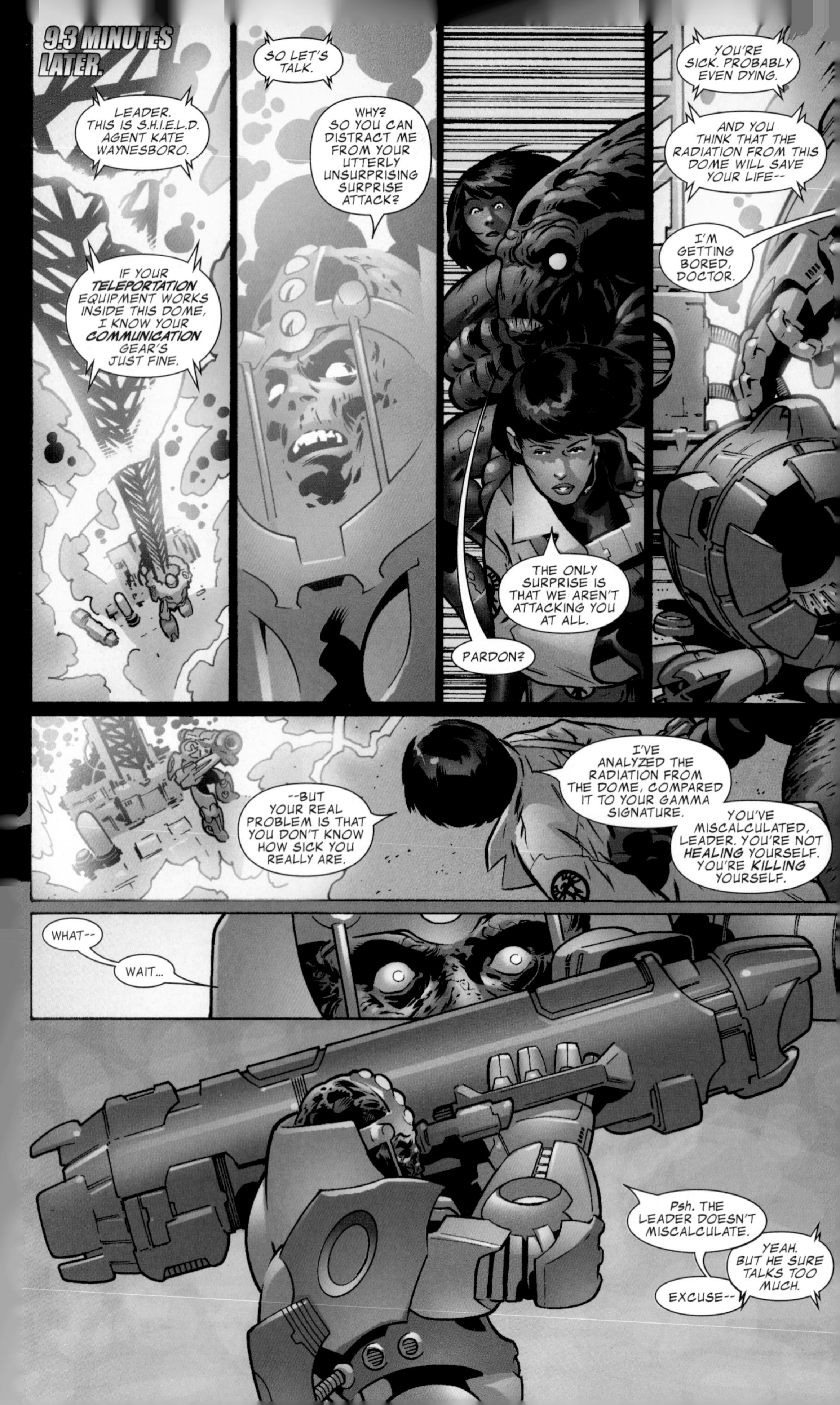
9.3 MINUTES LATER.
LEADER. THIS IS S.H.I.E.L.D. AGENT KATE WAYNESBORO.
IF YOUR TELEPORTATION EQUIPMENT WORKS INSIDE THIS DOME, I KNOW YOUR COMMUNICATION GEAR'S JUST FINE.
SO LET'S TALK.
WHY? SO YOU CAN DISTRACT ME FROM YOUR UTTERLY UNSURPRISING SURPRISE ATTACK?
THE ONLY SURPRISE IS THAT WE AREN'T ATTACKING YOU AT ALL.
PARDON?
YOU'RE SICK. PROBABLY EVEN DYING.
AND YOU THINK THAT THE RADIATION FROM THIS DOME WILL SAVE YOUR LIFE--
I'M GETTING BORED, DOCTOR.
--BUT YOUR REAL PROBLEM IS THAT YOU DON'T KNOW HOW SICK YOU REALLY ARE.
I'VE ANALYZED THE RADIATION FROM THE DOME, COMPARED IT TO YOUR GAMMA SIGNATURE.
YOU'VE MISCALCULATED, LEADER. YOU'RE NOT HEALING YOURSELF. YOU'RE KILLING YOURSELF.
WHAT--
WAIT...
Psh. THE LEADER DOESN'T MISCALCULATE.
EXCUSE--
YEAH. BUT HE SURE TALKS TOO MUCH.

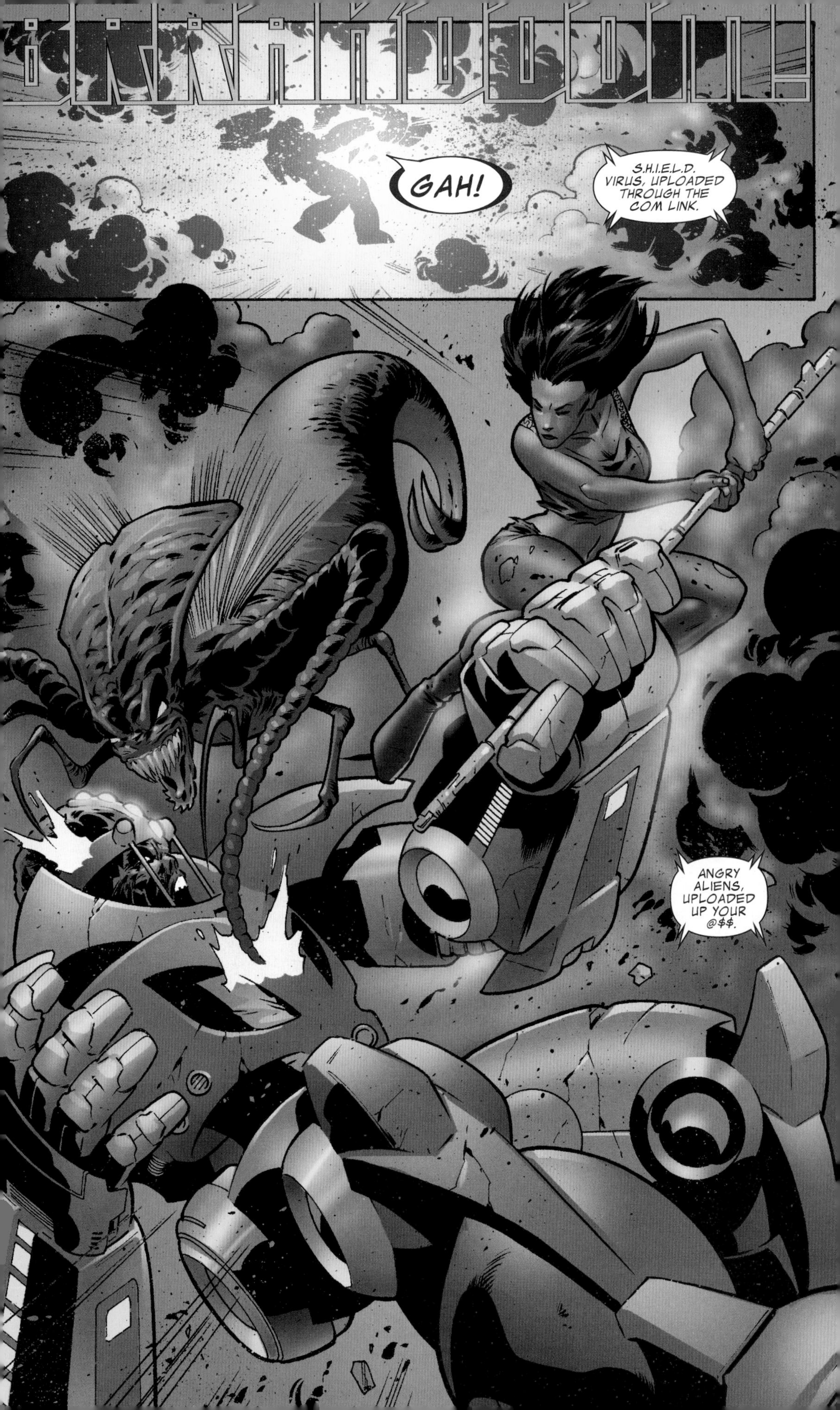
GAH!
S.H.I.E.L.D. VIRUS, UPLOADED THROUGH THE COM LINK.
ANGRY ALIENS, UPLOADED UP YOUR @$$.

THEN WHAT-- WAIT... NO.

ALL RIGHT. THERE'S YOUR DISTRACTION. WHERE DO WE DIG?

IT'S THE ONLY WAY, KORG. AND YOU'RE THE ONLY ONE STRONG ENOUGH.

ONCE I'M GONE, THE DOME LOSES ITS POWER.

I DIDN'T PUL YOU OUT OF THE MAGMA C SAKAAR TO KILL YOU HERE!

WE DON'T.

THERE'S NO GENERATING STATION. THE DOME FEEDS DIRECTLY ON THE OLD POWER THROUGH THE GROUND ITSELF.

IT'S THE ONLY HOPE THE HUMANS HAVE.

I DON'T--

I DON'T CARE ABOUT THE HUMANS!

THEN WHY DID YOU SWEAR TO PROTECT THEM?

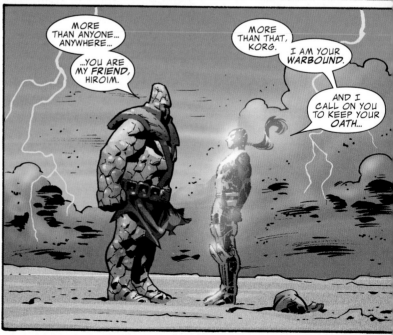

MORE THAN ANYONE... ANYWHERE...

...YOU ARE MY FRIEND, HIROIM.

MORE THAN THAT, KORG.

I AM YOUR WARBOUND.

AND I CALL ON YOU TO KEEP YOUR OATH...

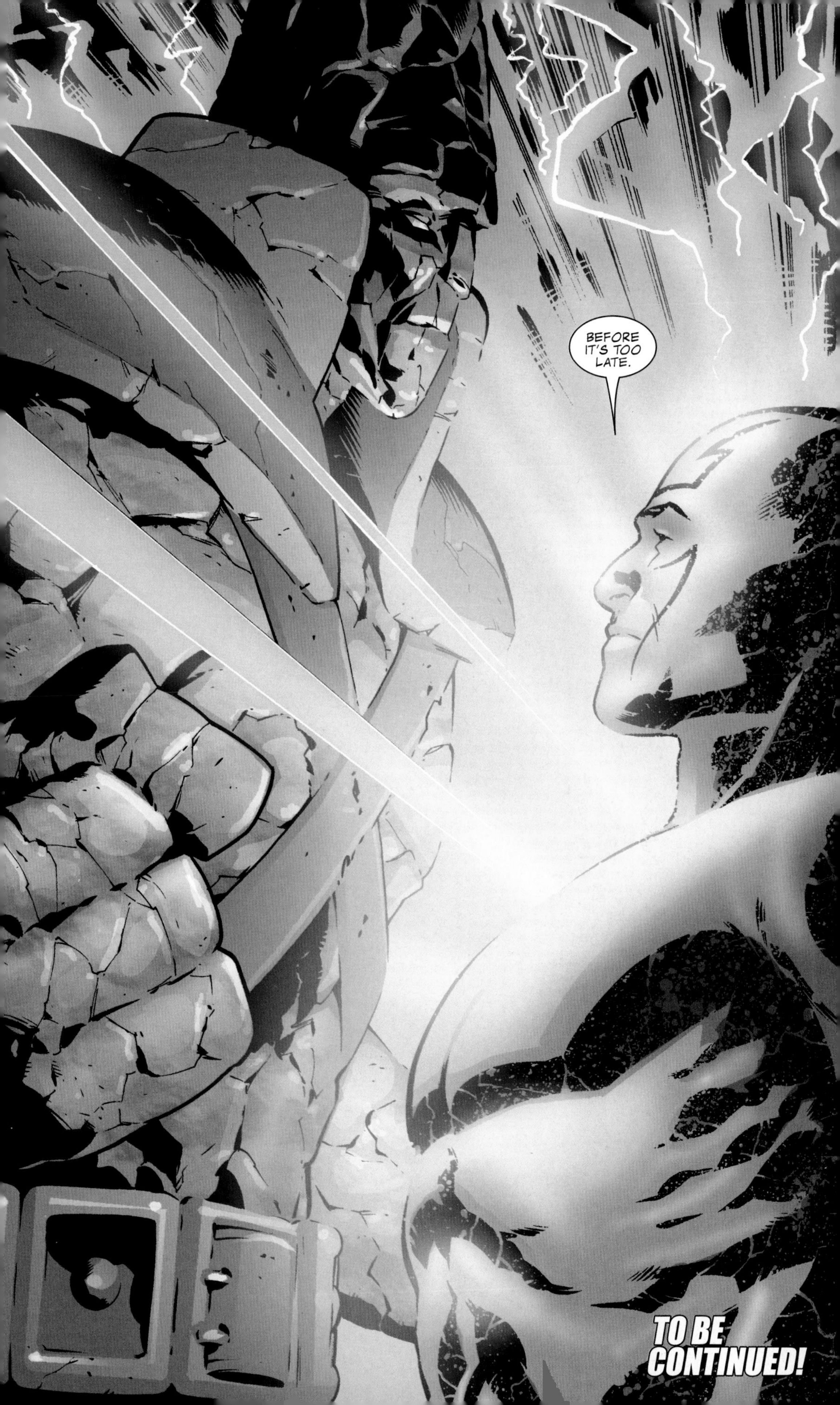
BEFORE IT'S TOO LATE.
TO BE CONTINUED!

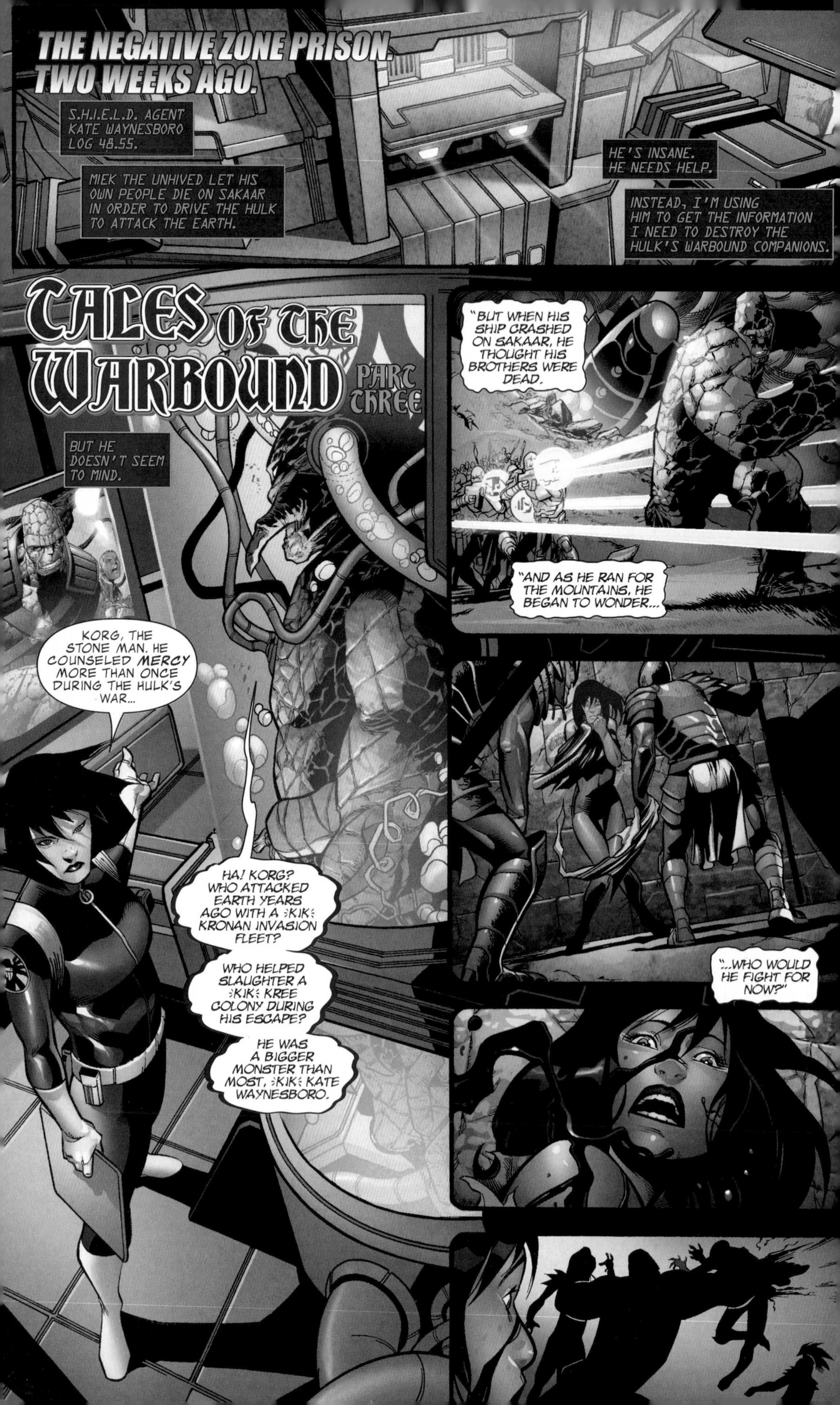
THE NEGATIVE ZONE PRISON. TWO WEEKS AGO.
S.H.I.E.L.D. AGENT KATE WAYNESBORO LOG 48.55.
MIEK THE UNHIVED LET HIS OWN PEOPLE DIE ON SAKAAR IN ORDER TO DRIVE THE HULK TO ATTACK THE EARTH.
HE'S INSANE. HE NEEDS HELP.
INSTEAD, I'M USING HIM TO GET THE INFORMATION I NEED TO DESTROY THE HULK'S WARBOUND COMPANIONS.
TALES OF THE WARBOUND PART THREE
BUT HE DOESN'T SEEM TO MIND.
KORG, THE STONE MAN. HE COUNSELED MERCY MORE THAN ONCE DURING THE HULK'S WAR...
HA! KORG? WHO ATTACKED EARTH YEARS AGO WITH A KIK KRONAN INVASION FLEET?
WHO HELPED SLAUGHTER A KIK KREE COLONY DURING HIS ESCAPE?
HE WAS A BIGGER MONSTER THAN MOST, KIK KATE WAYNESBORO.
"BUT WHEN HIS SHIP CRASHED ON SAKAAR, HE THOUGHT HIS BROTHERS WERE DEAD.
"AND AS HE RAN FOR THE MOUNTAINS, HE BEGAN TO WONDER...
"...WHO WOULD HE FIGHT FOR NOW?"

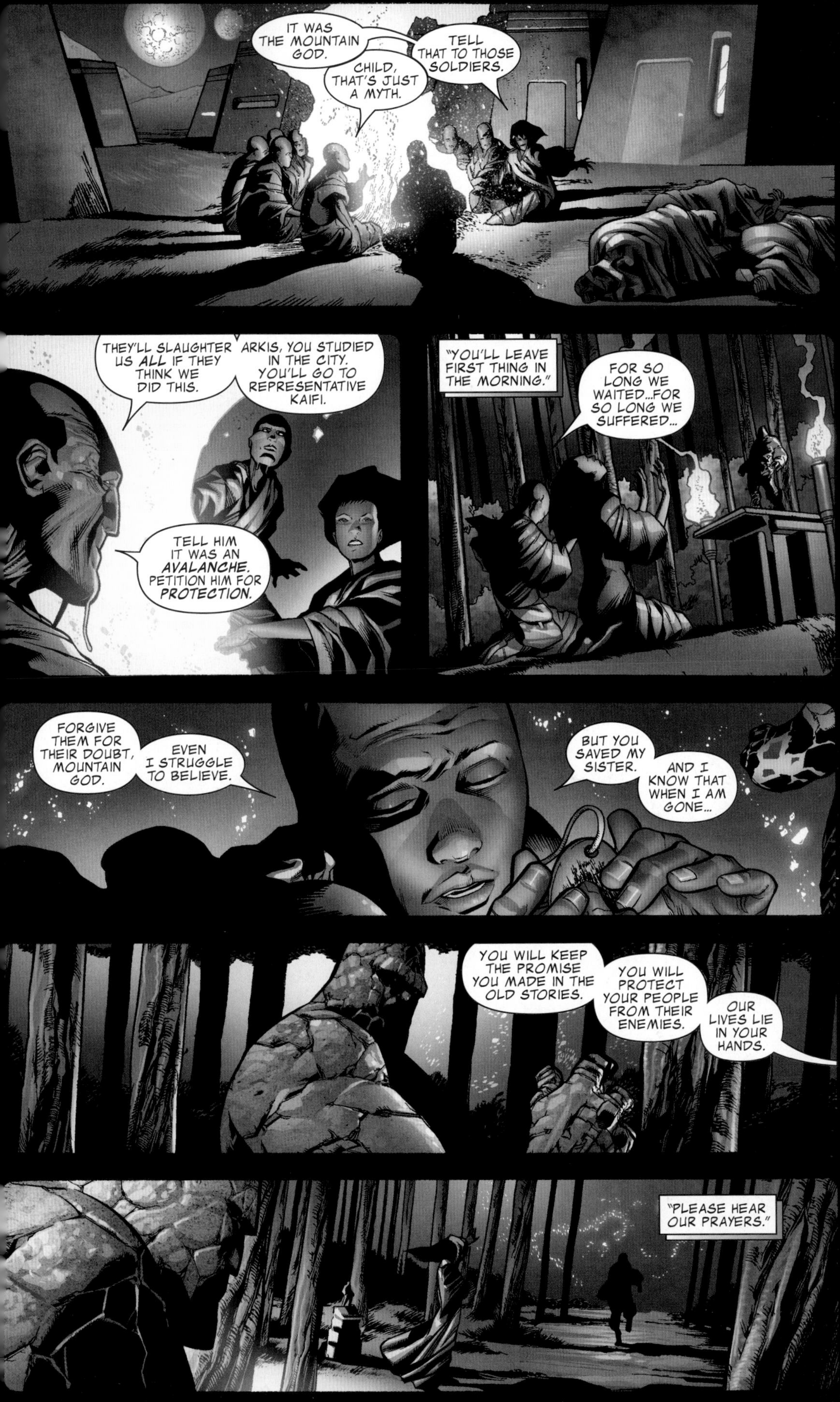

IT WAS THE MOUNTAIN GOD.
CHILD, THAT'S JUST A MYTH.
TELL THAT TO THOSE SOLDIERS.
THEY'LL SLAUGHTER US ALL IF THEY THINK WE DID THIS.
ARKIS, YOU STUDIED IN THE CITY. YOU'LL GO TO REPRESENTATIVE KAIFI.
TELL HIM IT WAS AN AVALANCHE. PETITION HIM FOR PROTECTION.
"YOU'LL LEAVE FIRST THING IN THE MORNING."
FOR SO LONG WE WAITED...FOR SO LONG WE SUFFERED...
FORGIVE THEM FOR THEIR DOUBT, MOUNTAIN GOD.
EVEN I STRUGGLE TO BELIEVE.
BUT YOU SAVED MY SISTER.
AND I KNOW THAT WHEN I AM GONE...
YOU WILL KEEP THE PROMISE YOU MADE IN THE OLD STORIES.
YOU WILL PROTECT YOUR PEOPLE FROM THEIR ENEMIES.
OUR LIVES LIE IN YOUR HANDS.
"PLEASE HEAR OUR PRAYERS."

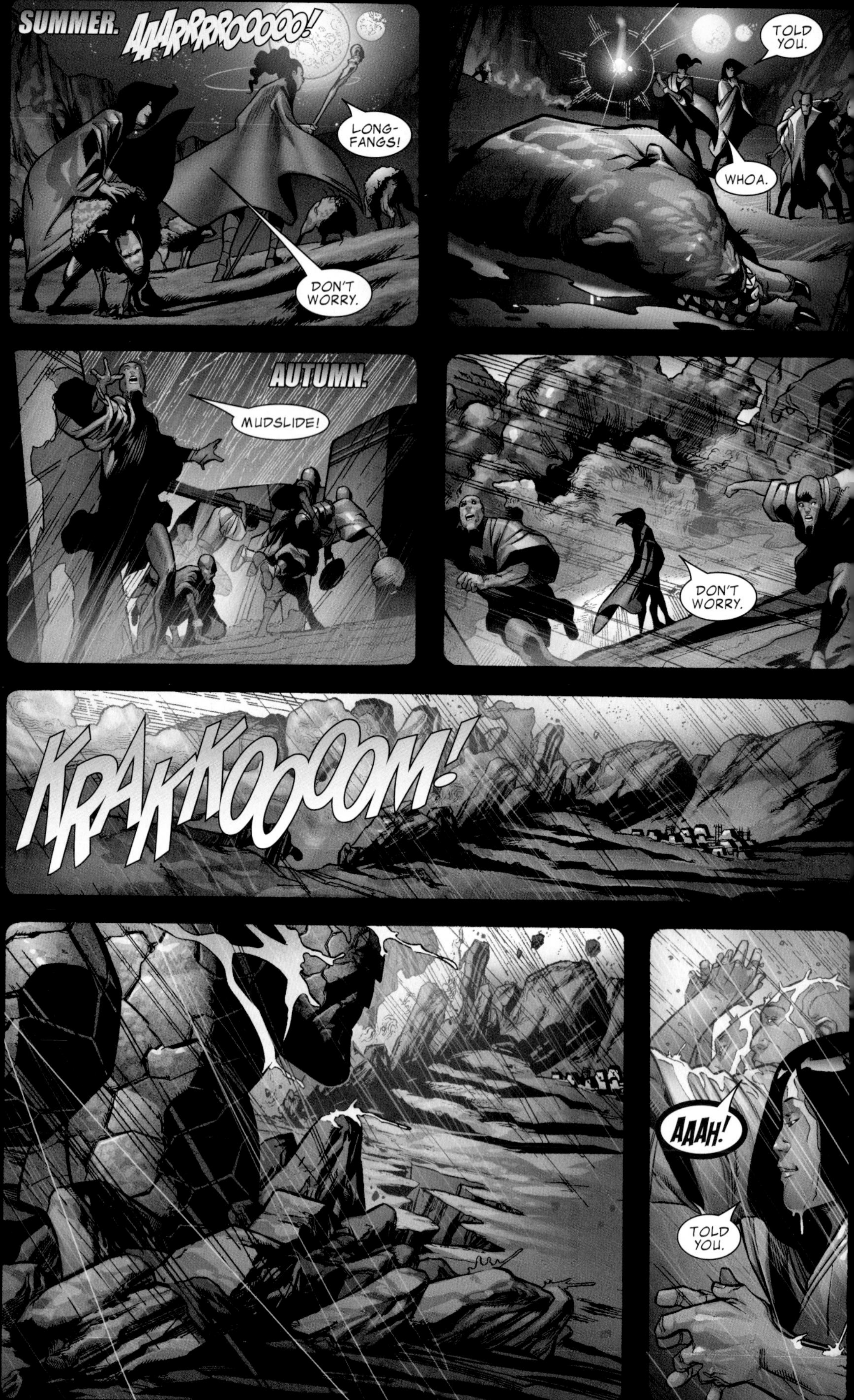
SUMMER.
AAARRRROOOOO!
LONG-FANGS!
DON'T WORRY.
TOLD YOU.
WHOA.
AUTUMN.
MUDSLIDE!
DON'T WORRY.
KRAKKOOOOM!
AAAH!
TOLD YOU.

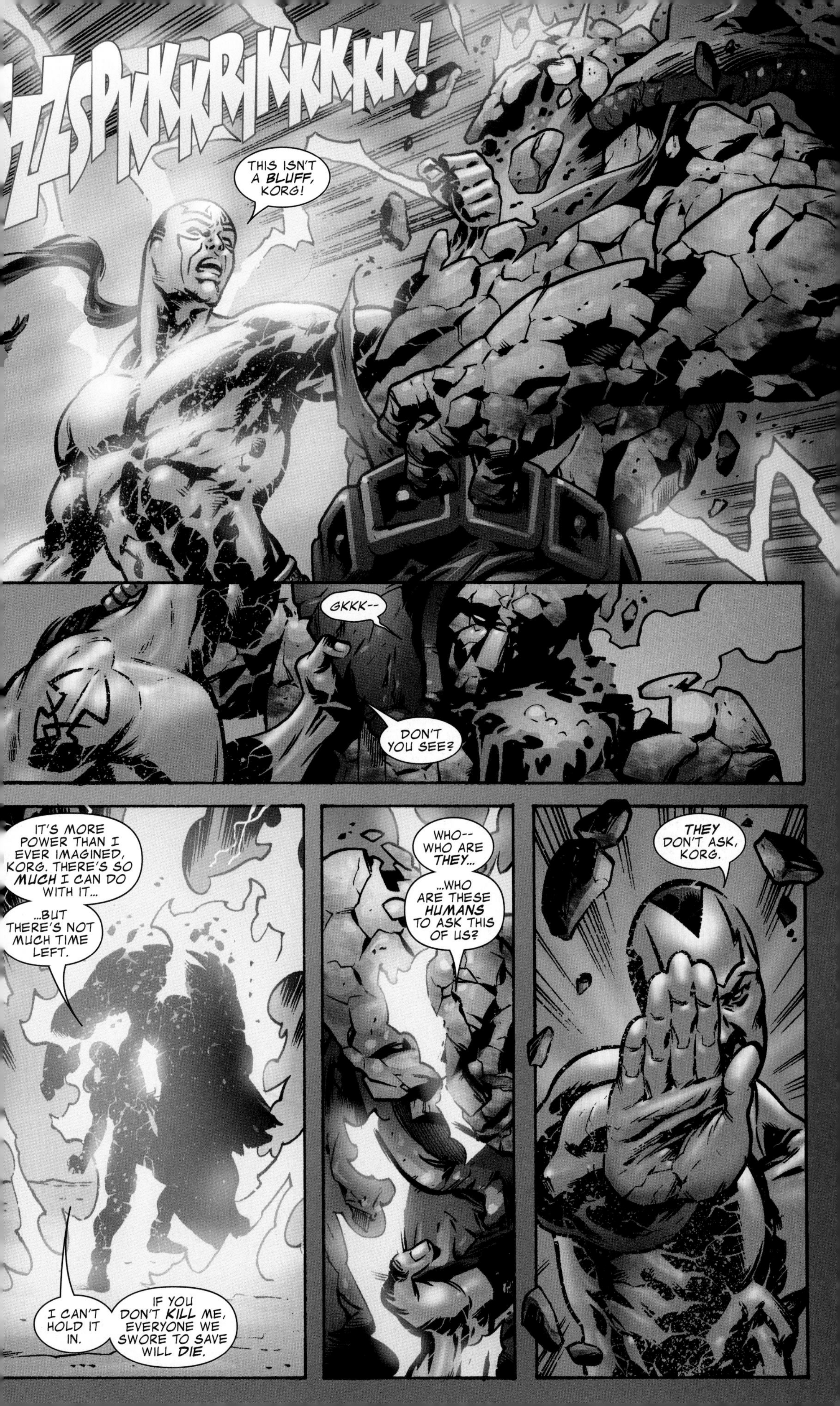
HZZSPKKKRIKKKKK!
THIS ISN'T A BLUFF, KORG!
GKKK--
DON'T YOU SEE?
IT'S MORE POWER THAN I EVER IMAGINED, KORG. THERE'S SO MUCH I CAN DO WITH IT...
...BUT THERE'S NOT MUCH TIME LEFT.
I CAN'T HOLD IT IN.
IF YOU DON'T KILL ME, EVERYONE WE SWORE TO SAVE WILL DIE.
WHO-- WHO ARE THEY...
...WHO ARE THESE HUMANS TO ASK THIS OF US?
THEY DON'T ASK, KORG.

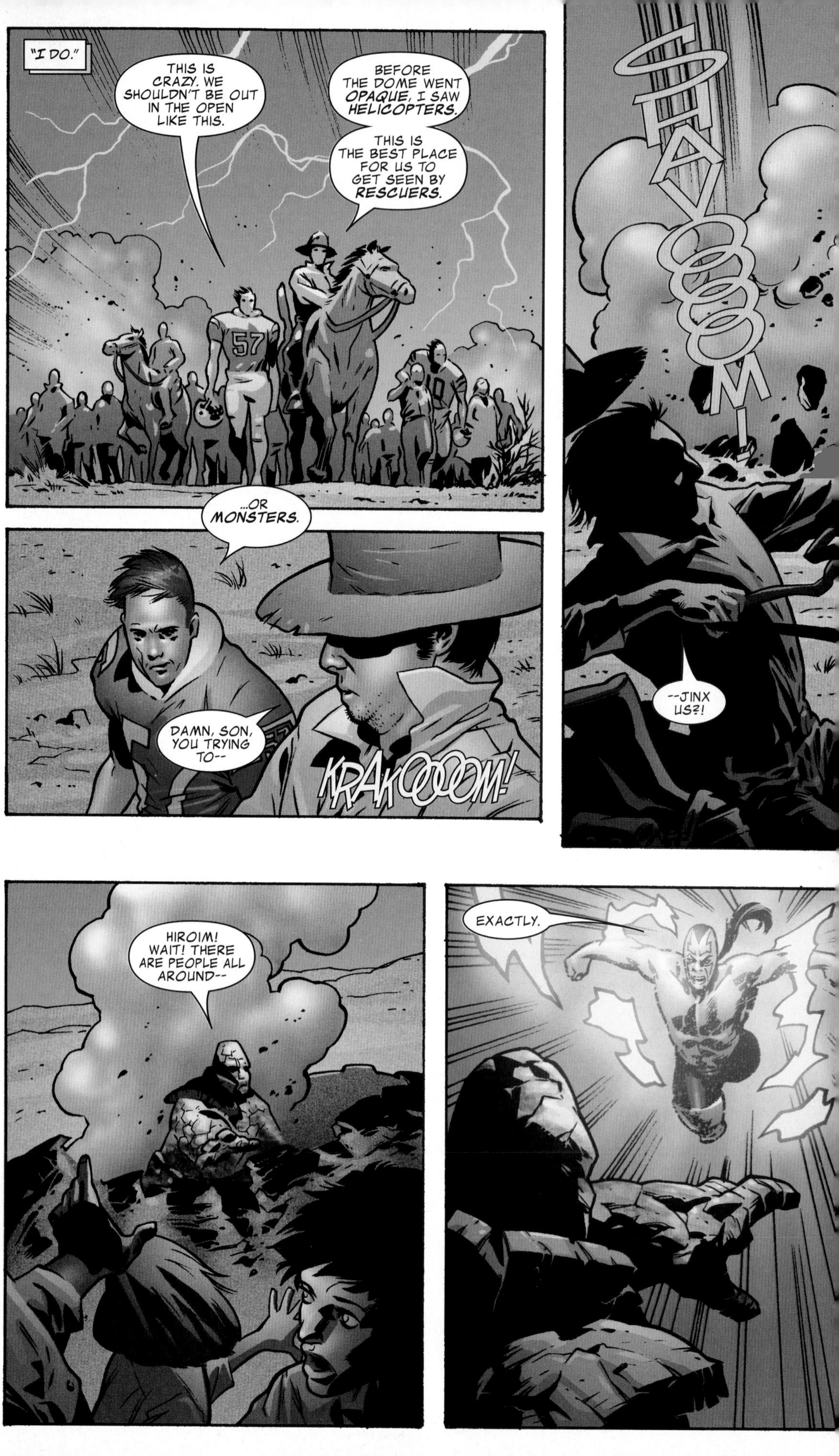
"I DO."
THIS IS CRAZY. WE SHOULDN'T BE OUT IN THE OPEN LIKE THIS.
BEFORE THE DOME WENT OPAQUE, I SAW HELICOPTERS.
THIS IS THE BEST PLACE FOR US TO GET SEEN BY RESCUERS.
...OR MONSTERS.
DAMN, SON, YOU TRYING TO--
KRAKOOOOM!
SHAVOOOOM!
--JINX US?!
HIROIM! WAIT! THERE ARE PEOPLE ALL AROUND--
EXACTLY.

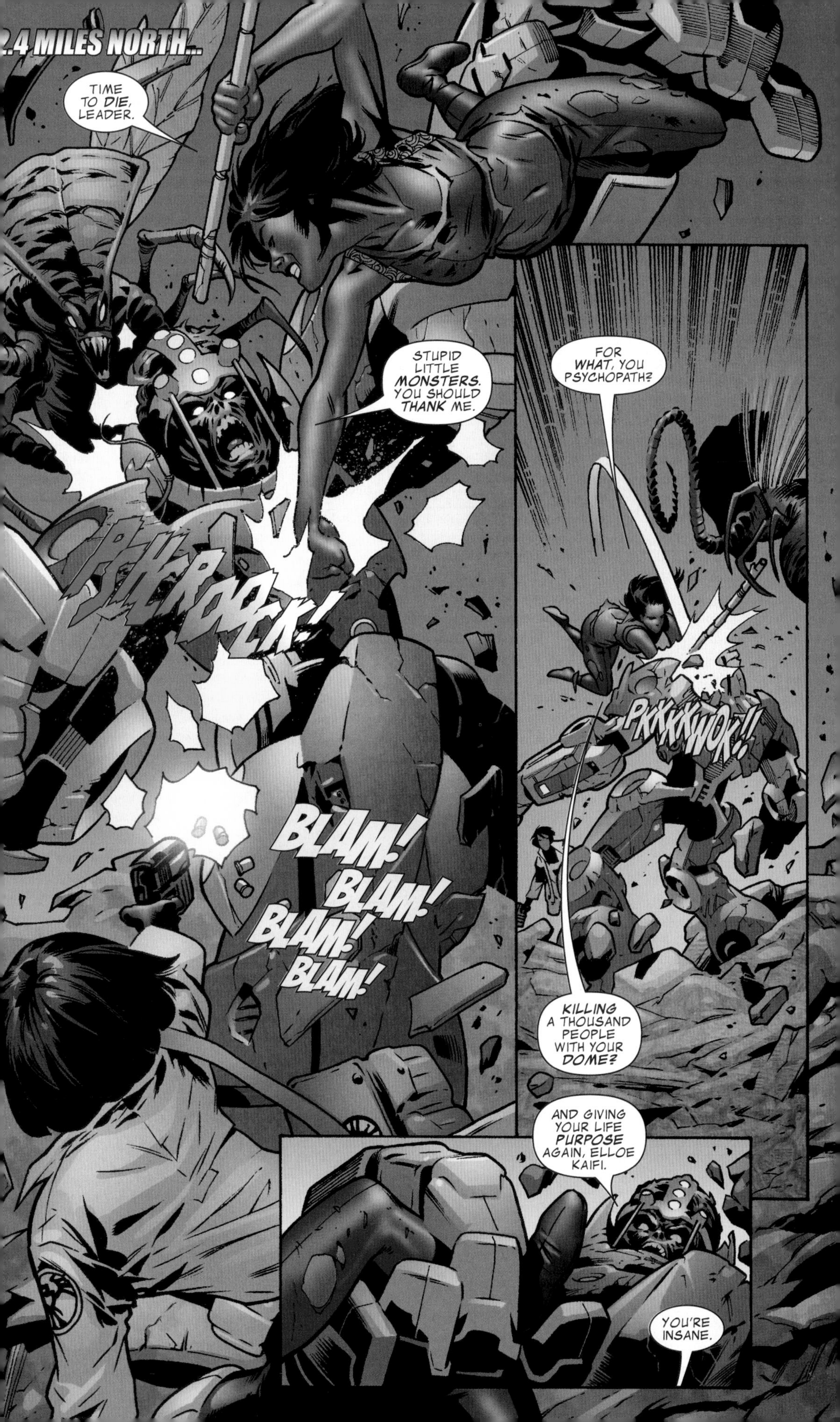

.4 MILES NORTH...
TIME TO DIE, LEADER.
STUPID LITTLE MONSTERS. YOU SHOULD THANK ME.
CPHROOCK!
BLAM! BLAM! BLAM! BLAM!
FOR WHAT, YOU PSYCHOPATH?
PKKKWOK!!
KILLING A THOUSAND PEOPLE WITH YOUR DOME?
AND GIVING YOUR LIFE PURPOSE AGAIN, ELLOE KAIFI.
YOU'RE INSANE.

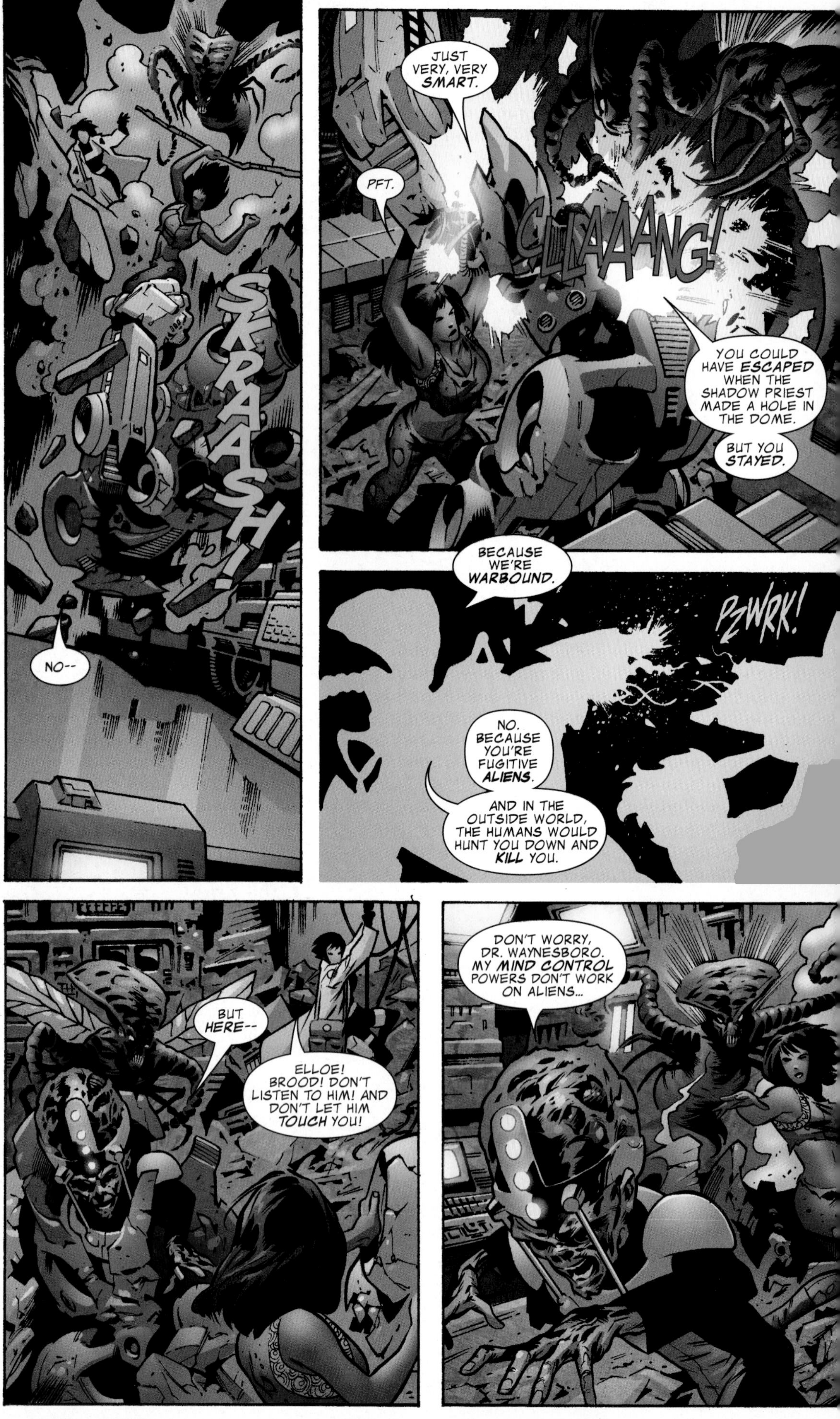
SKRAASH!
NO--
JUST VERY, VERY SMART.
PFT.
CLLAAAANG!
YOU COULD HAVE ESCAPED WHEN THE SHADOW PRIEST MADE A HOLE IN THE DOME.
BUT YOU STAYED.
BECAUSE WE'RE WARBOUND.
PZWRK!
NO. BECAUSE YOU'RE FUGITIVE ALIENS.
AND IN THE OUTSIDE WORLD, THE HUMANS WOULD HUNT YOU DOWN AND KILL YOU.
BUT HERE--
ELLOE! BROOD! DON'T LISTEN TO HIM! AND DON'T LET HIM TOUCH YOU!
DON'T WORRY, DR. WAYNESBORO. MY MIND CONTROL POWERS DON'T WORK ON ALIENS...

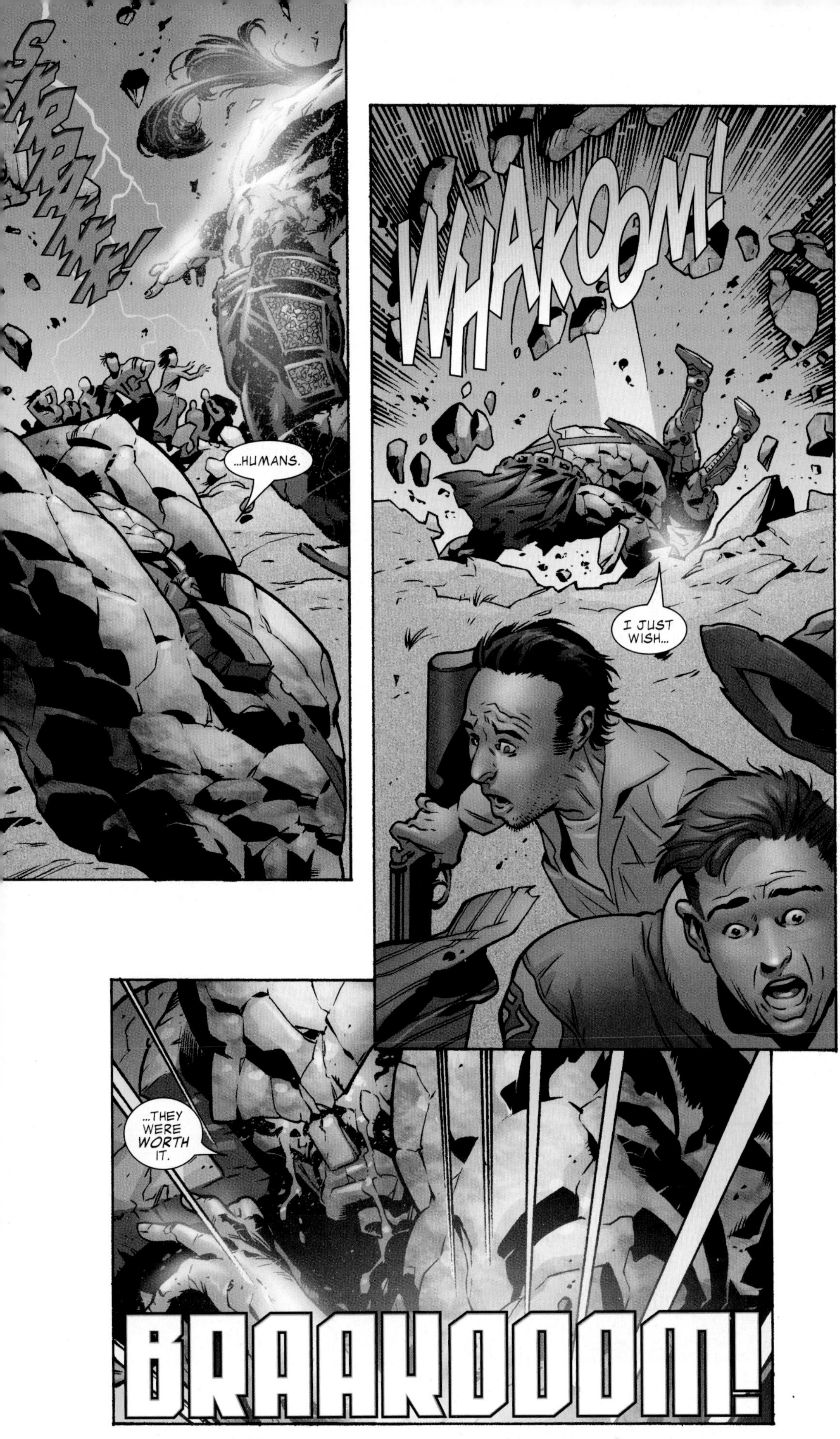
SHRAKKK!
...HUMANS.
WHAKOOM!
I JUST WISH...
...THEY WERE WORTH IT.
BRAAKOOOM!

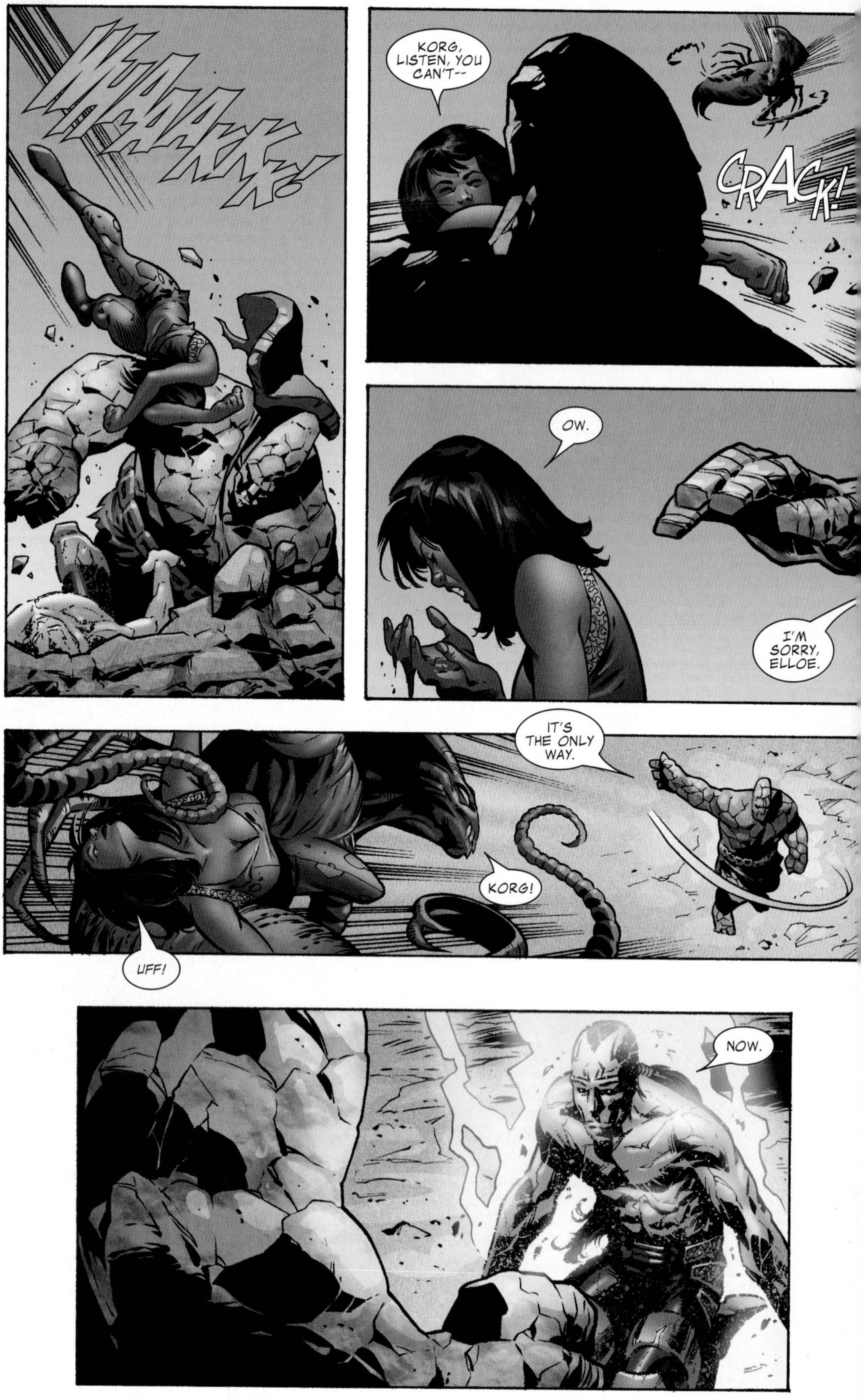
WHOOOMK!
KORG, LISTEN, YOU CAN'T--
CRACK!
OW.
I'M SORRY, ELLOE.
IT'S THE ONLY WAY.
KORG!
UFF!
NOW.

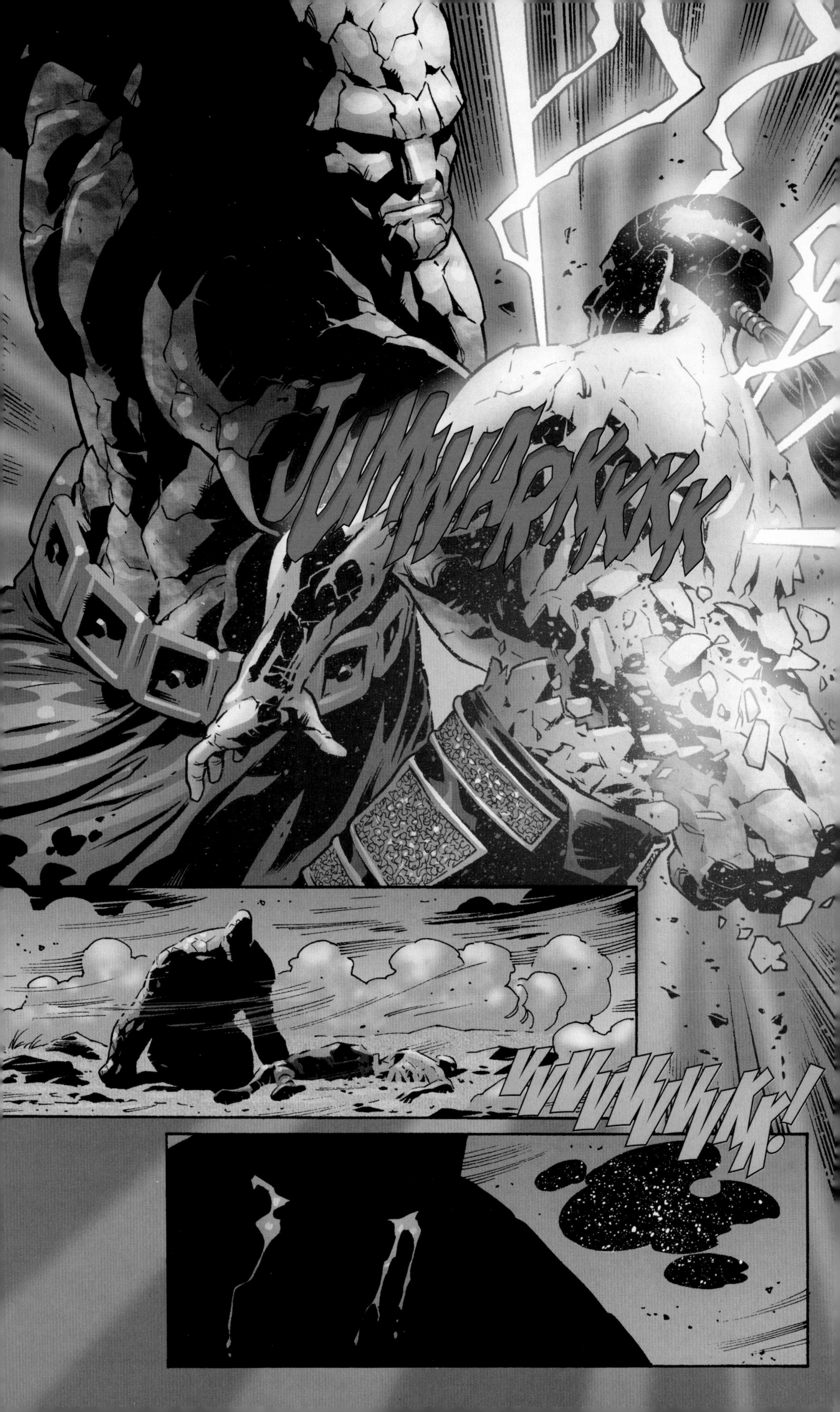

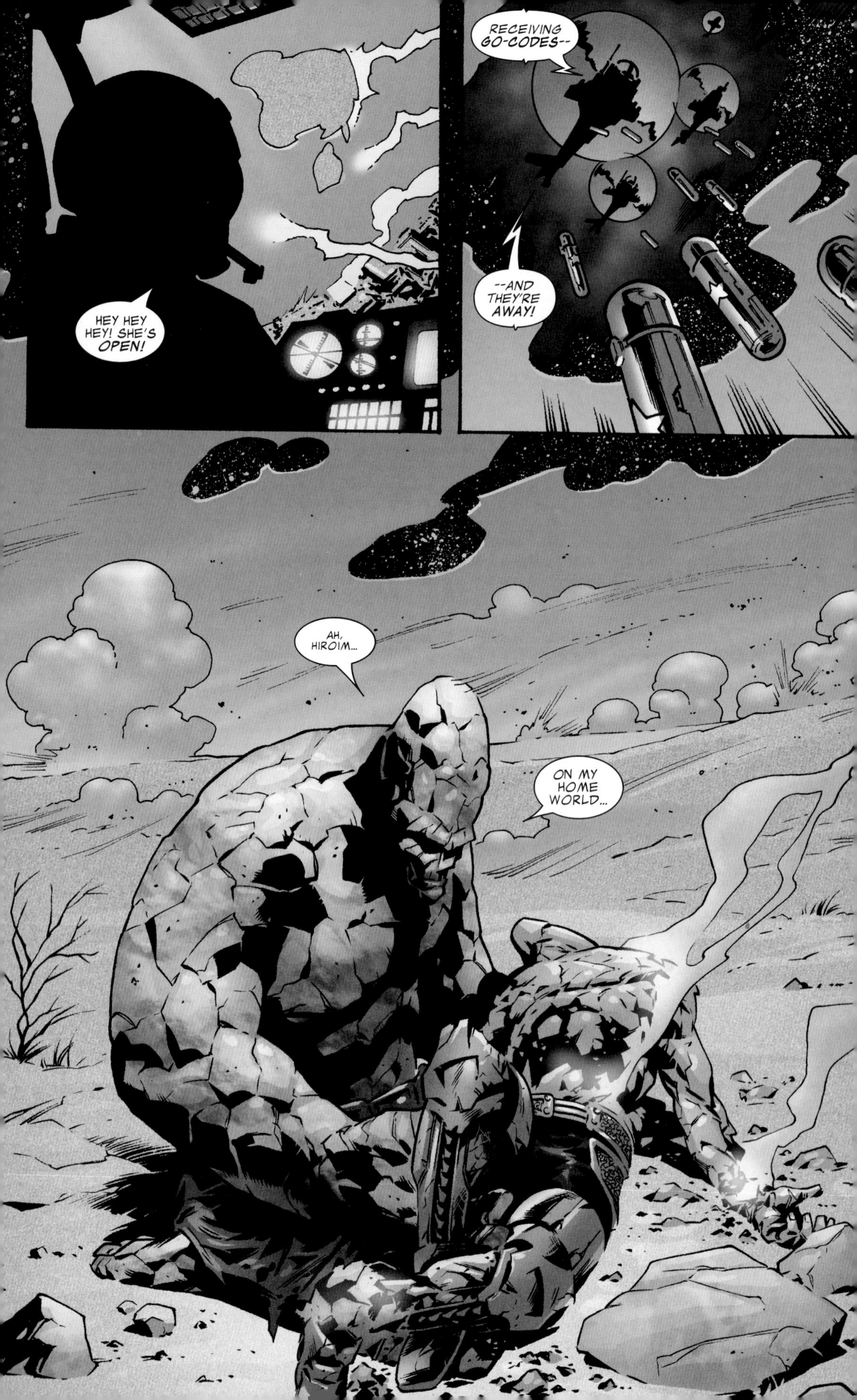
HEY HEY HEY! SHE'S OPEN!
RECEIVING GO-CODES--
--AND THEY'RE AWAY!
AH, HIROIM...
ON MY HOME WORLD...

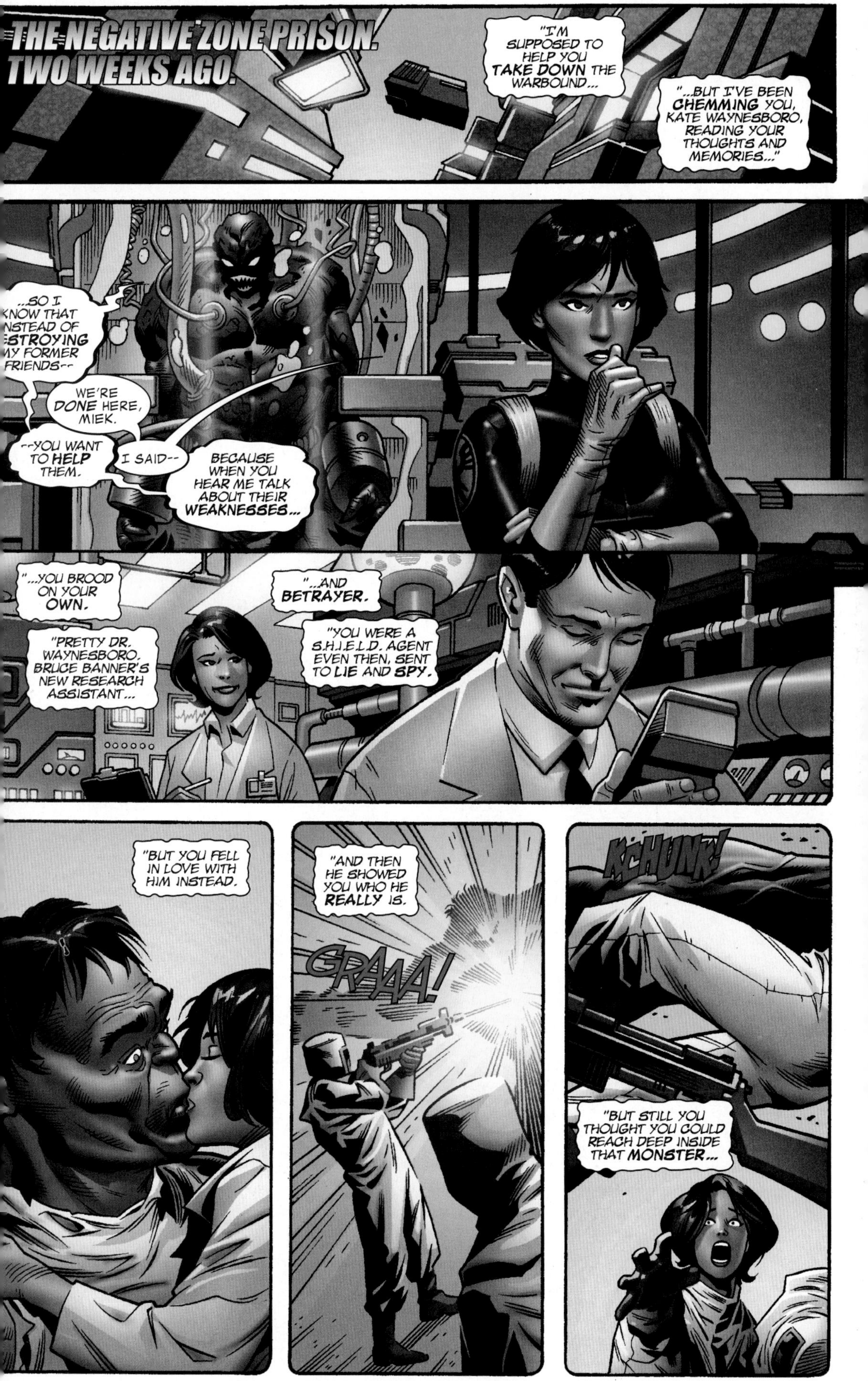
THE NEGATIVE ZONE PRISON. TWO WEEKS AGO.
"I'M SUPPOSED TO HELP YOU TAKE DOWN THE WARBOUND...
"...BUT I'VE BEEN CHEMMING YOU, KATE WAYNESBORO, READING YOUR THOUGHTS AND MEMORIES..."
...SO I KNOW THAT INSTEAD OF DESTROYING MY FORMER FRIENDS--
WE'RE DONE HERE, MIEK.
--YOU WANT TO HELP THEM.
I SAID--
BECAUSE WHEN YOU HEAR ME TALK ABOUT THEIR WEAKNESSES...
"...YOU BROOD ON YOUR OWN.
"PRETTY DR. WAYNESBORO, BRUCE BANNER'S NEW RESEARCH ASSISTANT...
"...AND BETRAYER.
"YOU WERE A S.H.I.E.L.D. AGENT EVEN THEN, SENT TO LIE AND SPY.
"BUT YOU FELL IN LOVE WITH HIM INSTEAD.
"AND THEN HE SHOWED YOU WHO HE REALLY IS.
GRAAA!
KCHUNK!
"BUT STILL YOU THOUGHT YOU COULD REACH DEEP INSIDE THAT MONSTER...

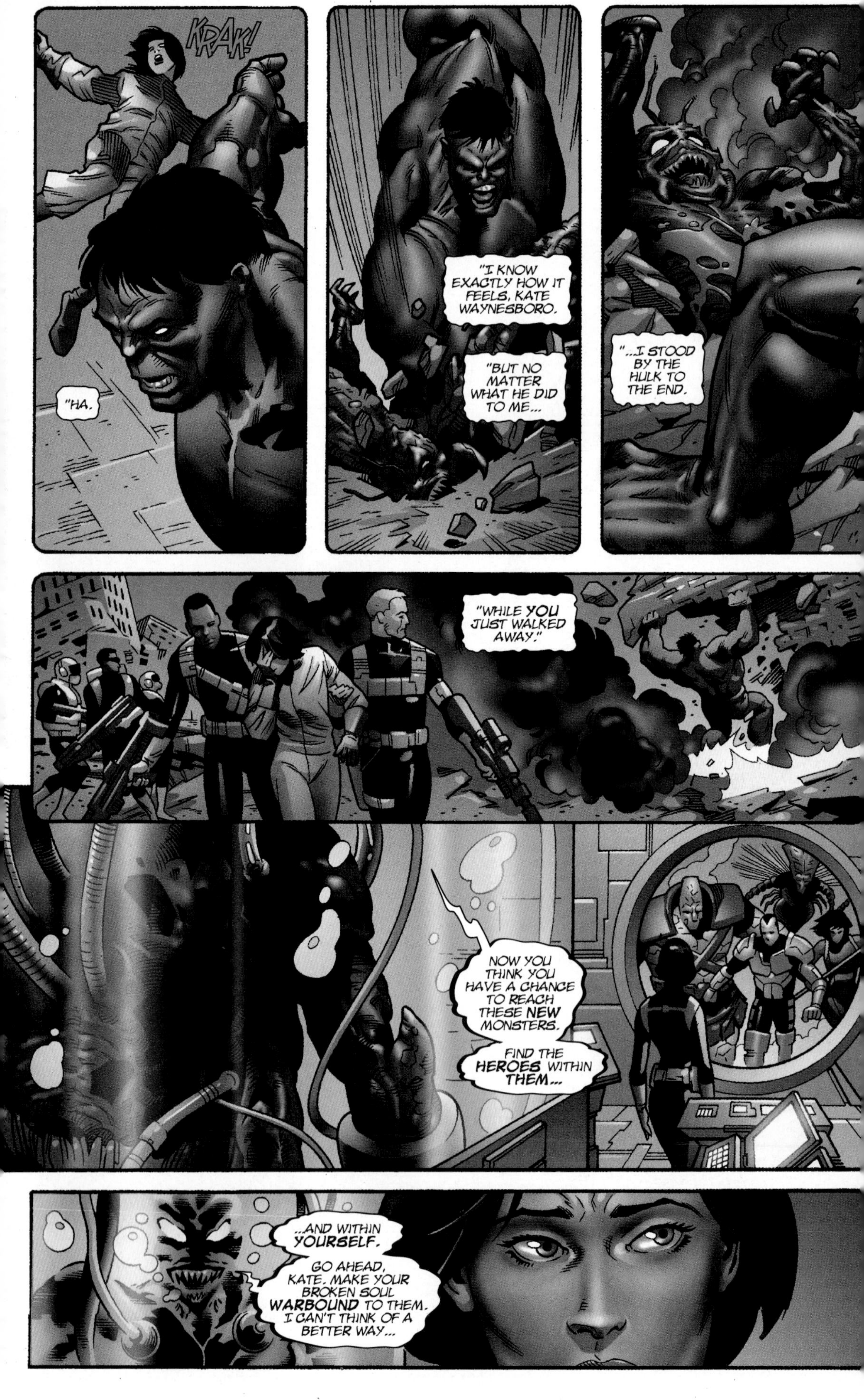
KRAK!
"HA.
"I KNOW EXACTLY HOW IT FEELS, KATE WAYNESBORO.
"BUT NO MATTER WHAT HE DID TO ME...
"...I STOOD BY THE HULK TO THE END.
"WHILE YOU JUST WALKED AWAY."
NOW YOU THINK YOU HAVE A CHANCE TO REACH THESE NEW MONSTERS.
FIND THE HEROES WITHIN THEM...
...AND WITHIN YOURSELF.
GO AHEAD, KATE. MAKE YOUR BROKEN SOUL WARBOUND TO THEM. I CAN'T THINK OF A BETTER WAY...

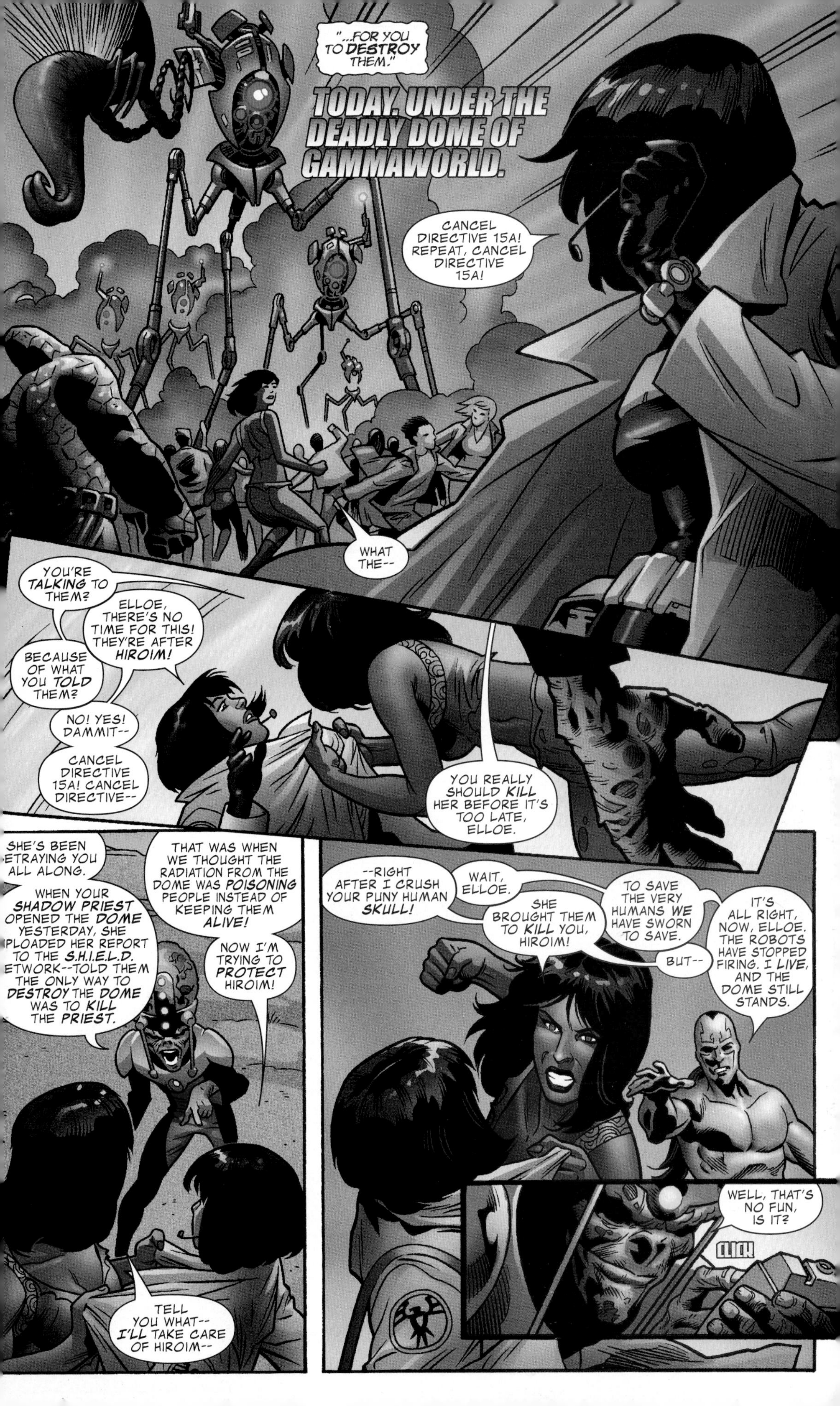
"...FOR YOU TO DESTROY THEM."
TODAY. UNDER THE DEADLY DOME OF GAMMAWORLD.
CANCEL DIRECTIVE 15A! REPEAT, CANCEL DIRECTIVE 15A!
WHAT THE--
YOU'RE TALKING TO THEM?
ELLOE, THERE'S NO TIME FOR THIS! THEY'RE AFTER HIROIM!
BECAUSE OF WHAT YOU TOLD THEM?
NO! YES! DAMMIT--
CANCEL DIRECTIVE 15A! CANCEL DIRECTIVE--
YOU REALLY SHOULD KILL HER BEFORE IT'S TOO LATE, ELLOE.
SHE'S BEEN ETRAYING YOU ALL ALONG.
WHEN YOUR SHADOW PRIEST OPENED THE DOME YESTERDAY, SHE PLOADED HER REPORT TO THE S.H.I.E.L.D. ETWORK--TOLD THEM THE ONLY WAY TO DESTROY THE DOME WAS TO KILL THE PRIEST.
THAT WAS WHEN WE THOUGHT THE RADIATION FROM THE DOME WAS POISONING PEOPLE INSTEAD OF KEEPING THEM ALIVE!
NOW I'M TRYING TO PROTECT HIROIM!
TELL YOU WHAT-- I'LL TAKE CARE OF HIROIM--
--RIGHT AFTER I CRUSH YOUR PUNY HUMAN SKULL!
WAIT, ELLOE.
SHE BROUGHT THEM TO KILL YOU, HIROIM!
TO SAVE THE VERY HUMANS WE HAVE SWORN TO SAVE.
BUT--
IT'S ALL RIGHT, NOW, ELLOE. THE ROBOTS HAVE STOPPED FIRING. I LIVE, AND THE DOME STILL STANDS.
WELL, THAT'S NO FUN, IS IT?
CLICK

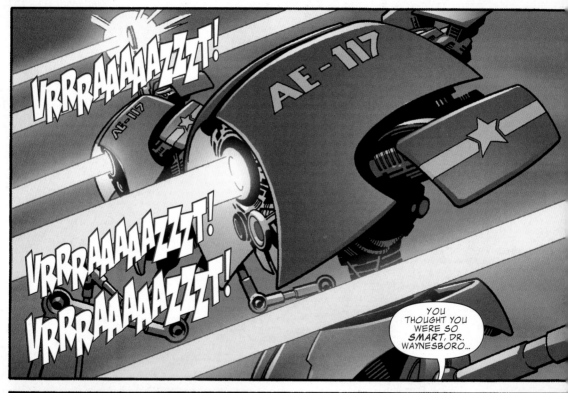

VRRRAAAAZZZT!

VRRRAAAAZZZT!

VRRRAAAAZZZT!

AE - 117

YOU THOUGHT YOU WERE SO *SMART*, DR. WAYNESBORO...

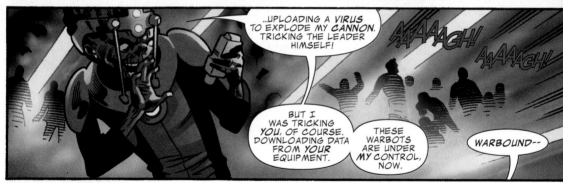

...UPLOADING A *VIRUS* TO EXPLODE MY *CANNON*. TRICKING THE LEADER HIMSELF!

AAAAAGH!

AAAAAGH!

BUT I WAS TRICKING *YOU*, OF COURSE. DOWNLOADING DATA FROM *YOUR* EQUIPMENT.

THESE *WARBOTS* ARE UNDER *MY* CONTROL, NOW.

WARBOUND--

--SMAAASH!

HIROIM! WAIT! THESE MACHINES--YOU CAN'T USE YOUR OLD POWER ON THEM!

HIROIM! YOU HAVE TO LISTEN TO ME! THEY'RE DESIGNED TO--

AAAAAGH!

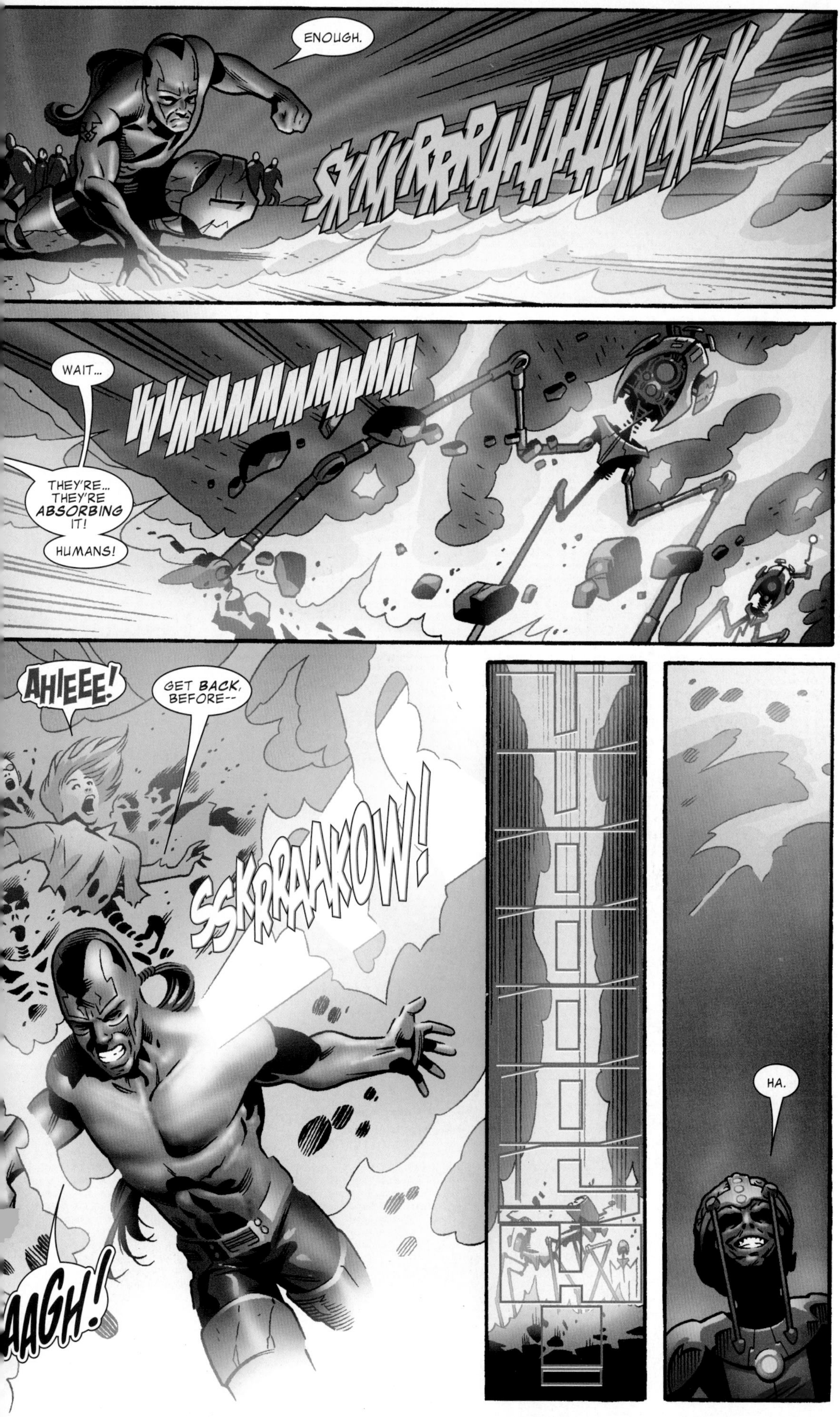
ENOUGH.
SKKKRRRAAAAAKKKKK
WAIT...
VVVMMMMMMMMMM
THEY'RE... THEY'RE ABSORBING IT!
HUMANS!
AHIEEE!
GET BACK, BEFORE--
SSKRRAAKOW!
AAGH!
HA.

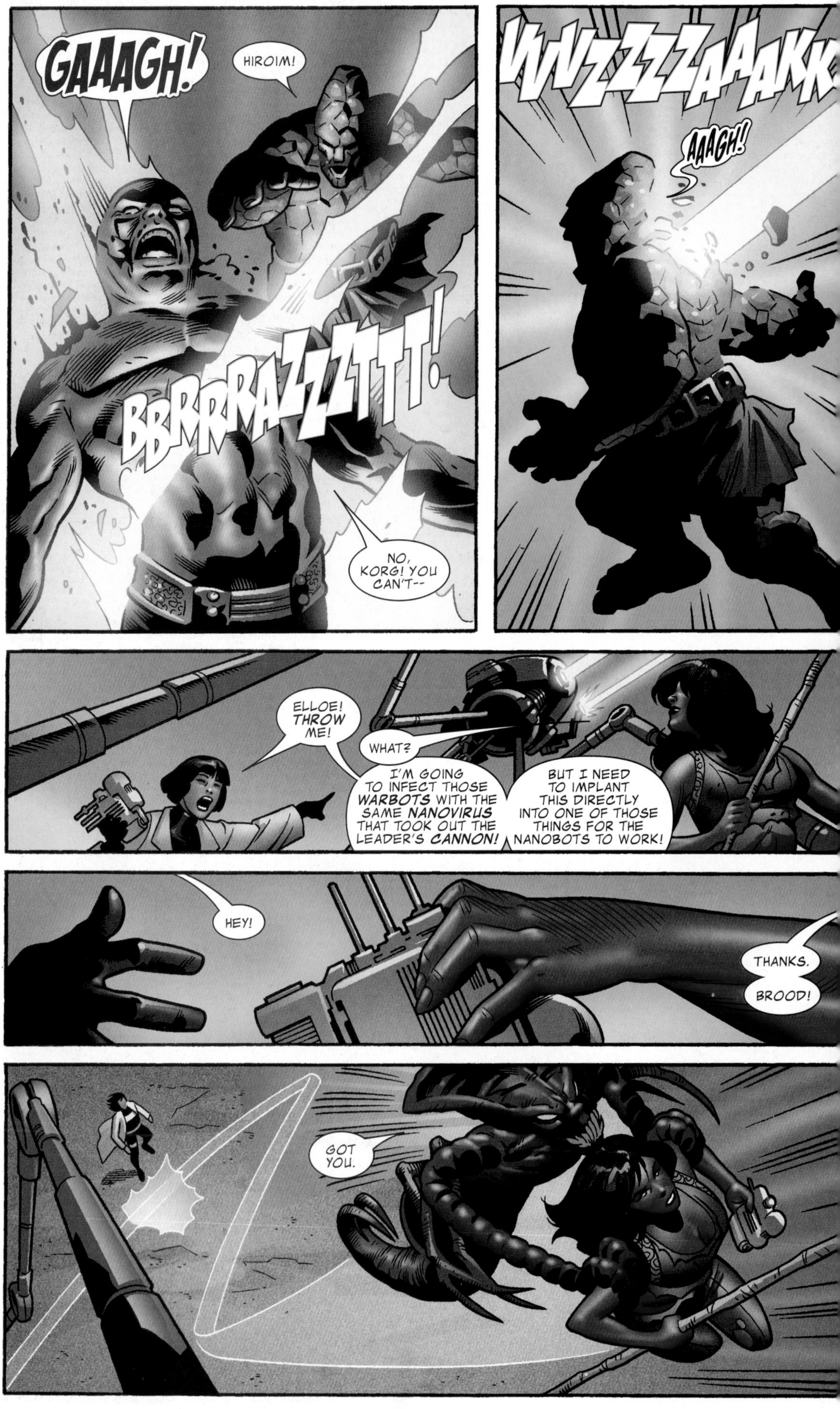
GAAAGH!
HIROIM!
BBRRRAZZZTTTT!
NO, KORG! YOU CAN'T--
VVVZZZZAAAKK
AAAGH!
ELLOE! THROW ME!
WHAT?
I'M GOING TO INFECT THOSE WARBOTS WITH THE SAME NANOVIRUS THAT TOOK OUT THE LEADER'S CANNON!
BUT I NEED TO IMPLANT THIS DIRECTLY INTO ONE OF THOSE THINGS FOR THE NANOBOTS TO WORK!
HEY!
THANKS.
BROOD!
GOT YOU.

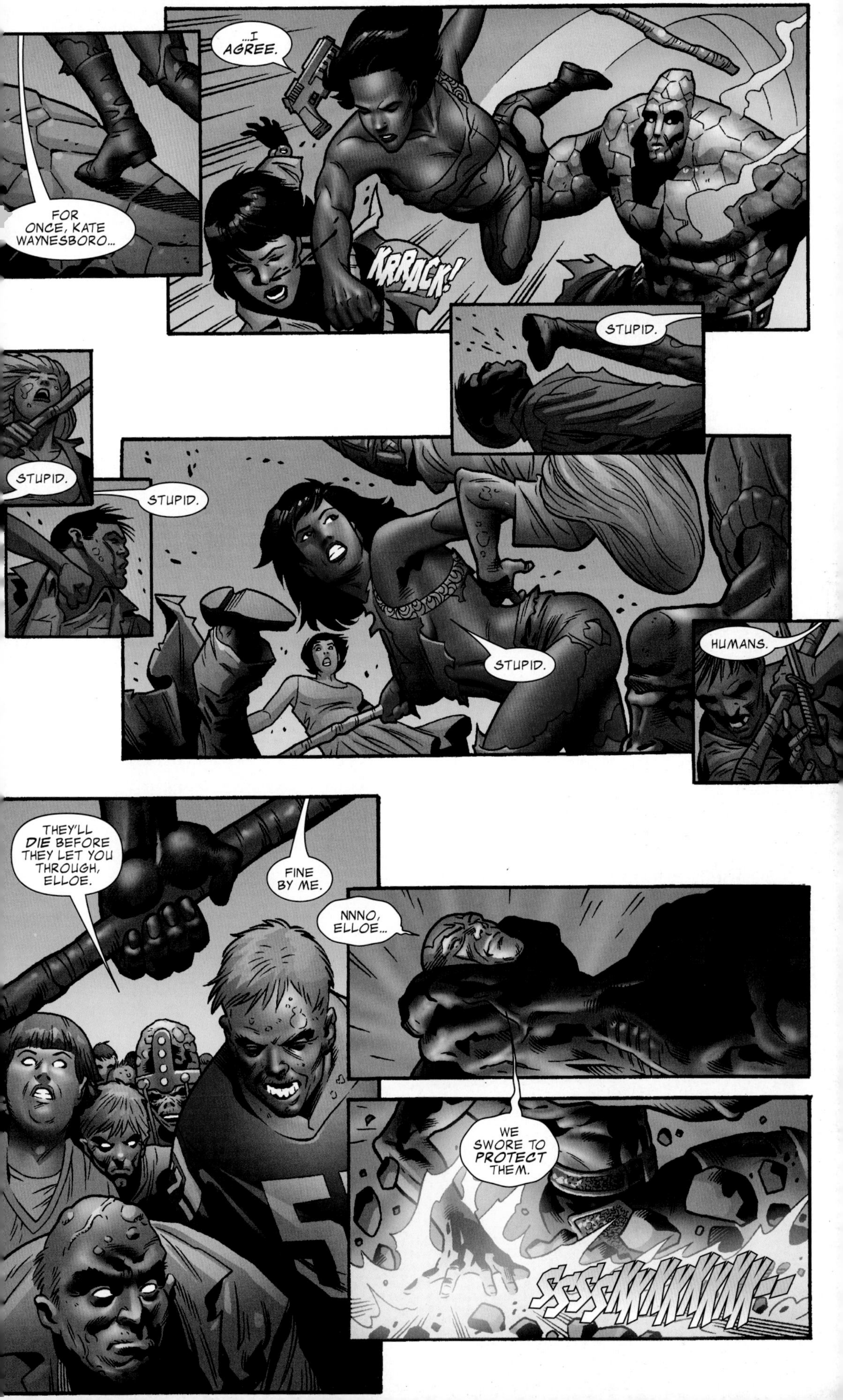
FOR ONCE, KATE WAYNESBORO...
...I AGREE.
KRRACK!
STUPID.
STUPID.
STUPID.
STUPID.
HUMANS.
THEY'LL *DIE* BEFORE THEY LET YOU THROUGH, ELLOE.
FINE BY ME.
NNNO, ELLOE...
WE SWORE TO *PROTECT* THEM.
SSSKKKKKKKKK-

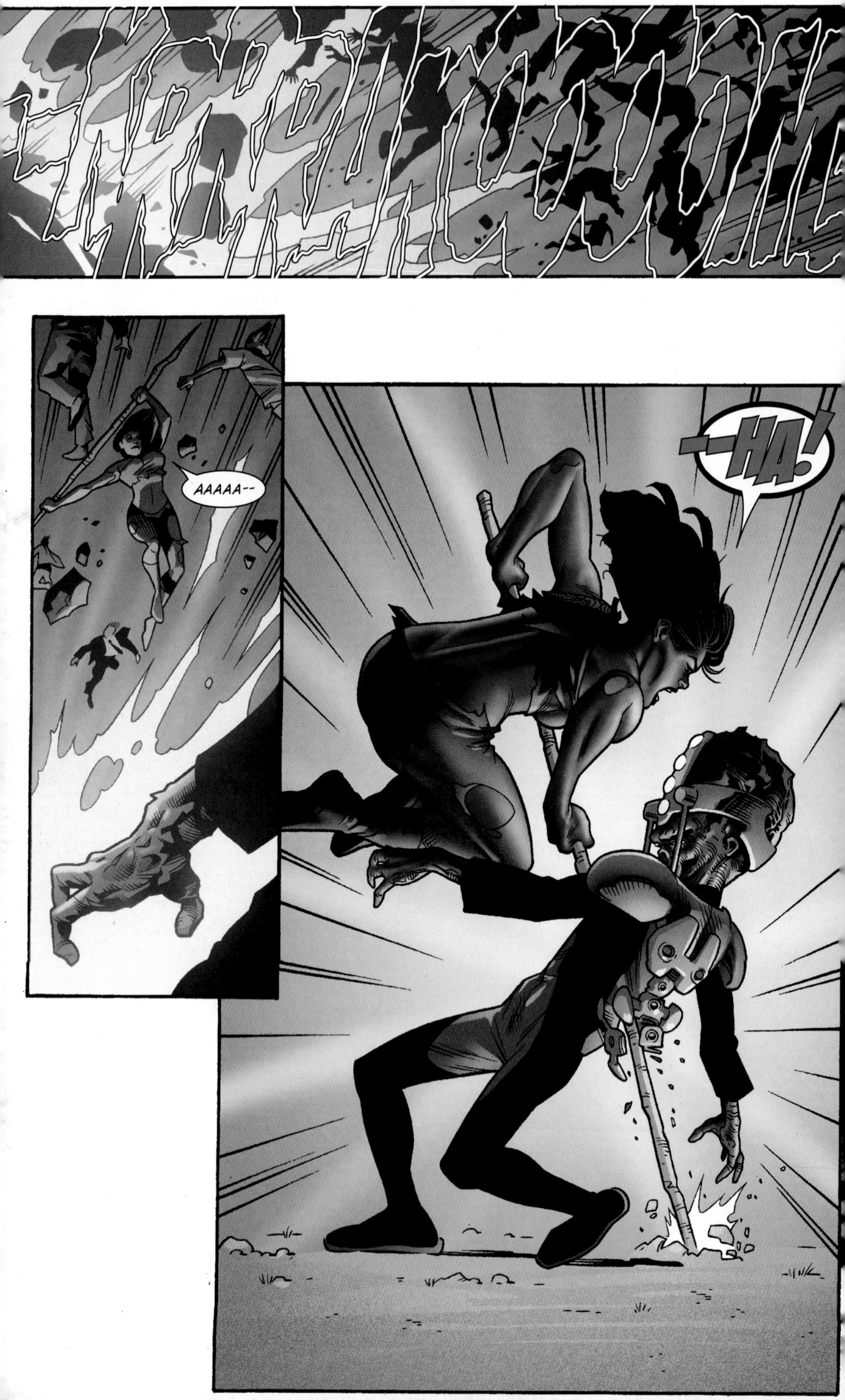
AAAAA--
--HA!

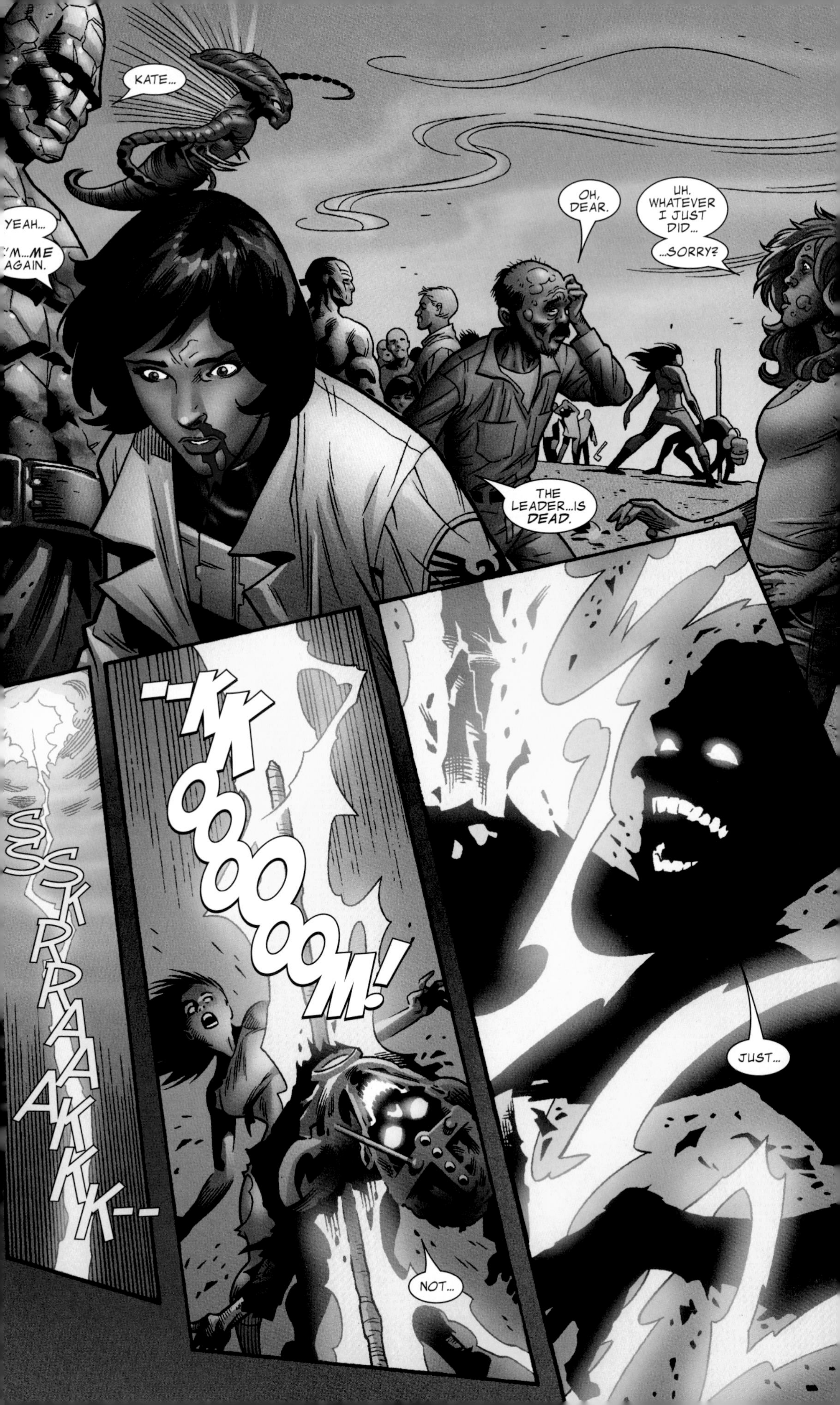

KATE...
YEAH... I'M...ME AGAIN.
OH, DEAR.
UH. WHATEVER I JUST DID...
...SORRY?
THE LEADER...IS DEAD.
SSSKRRAAAKKK--
--KKOOOOOOM!
JUST...
NOT...

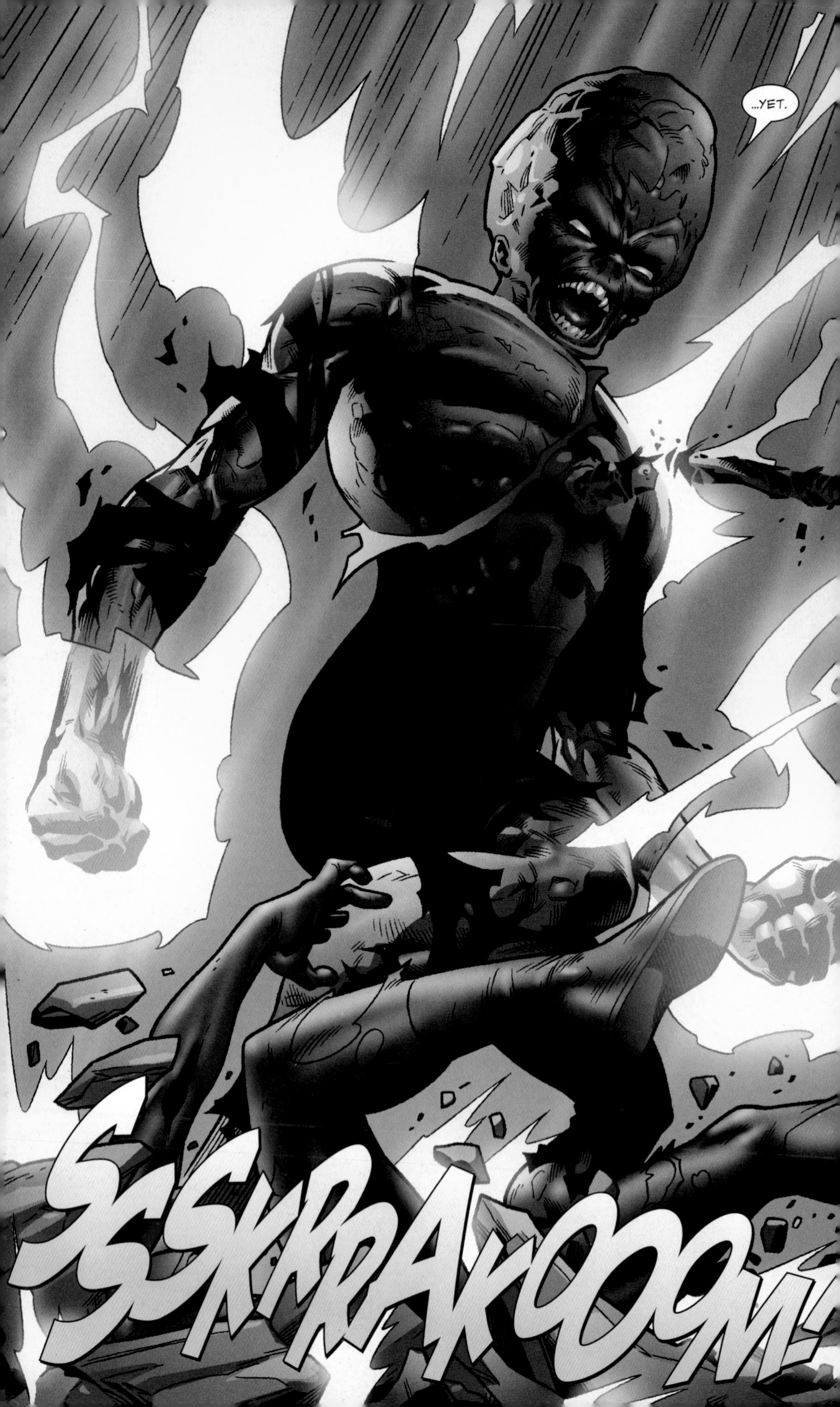
...YET.
SSKRRAKOOOM!

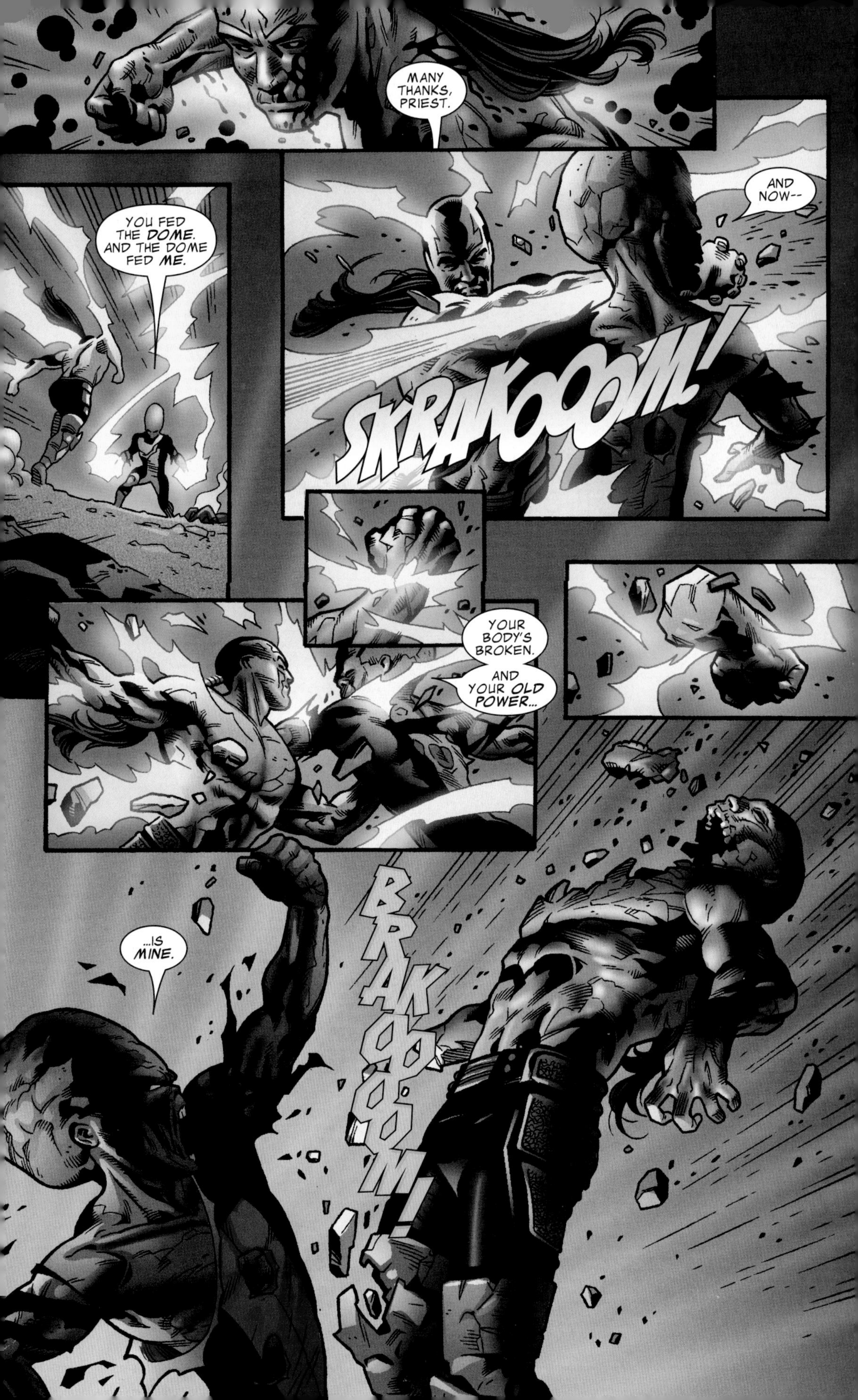
MANY THANKS, PRIEST.
YOU FED THE DOME. AND THE DOME FED ME.
AND NOW--
SKRAKOOOM!
YOUR BODY'S BROKEN.
AND YOUR OLD POWER...
...IS MINE.
BRAKOOOM!

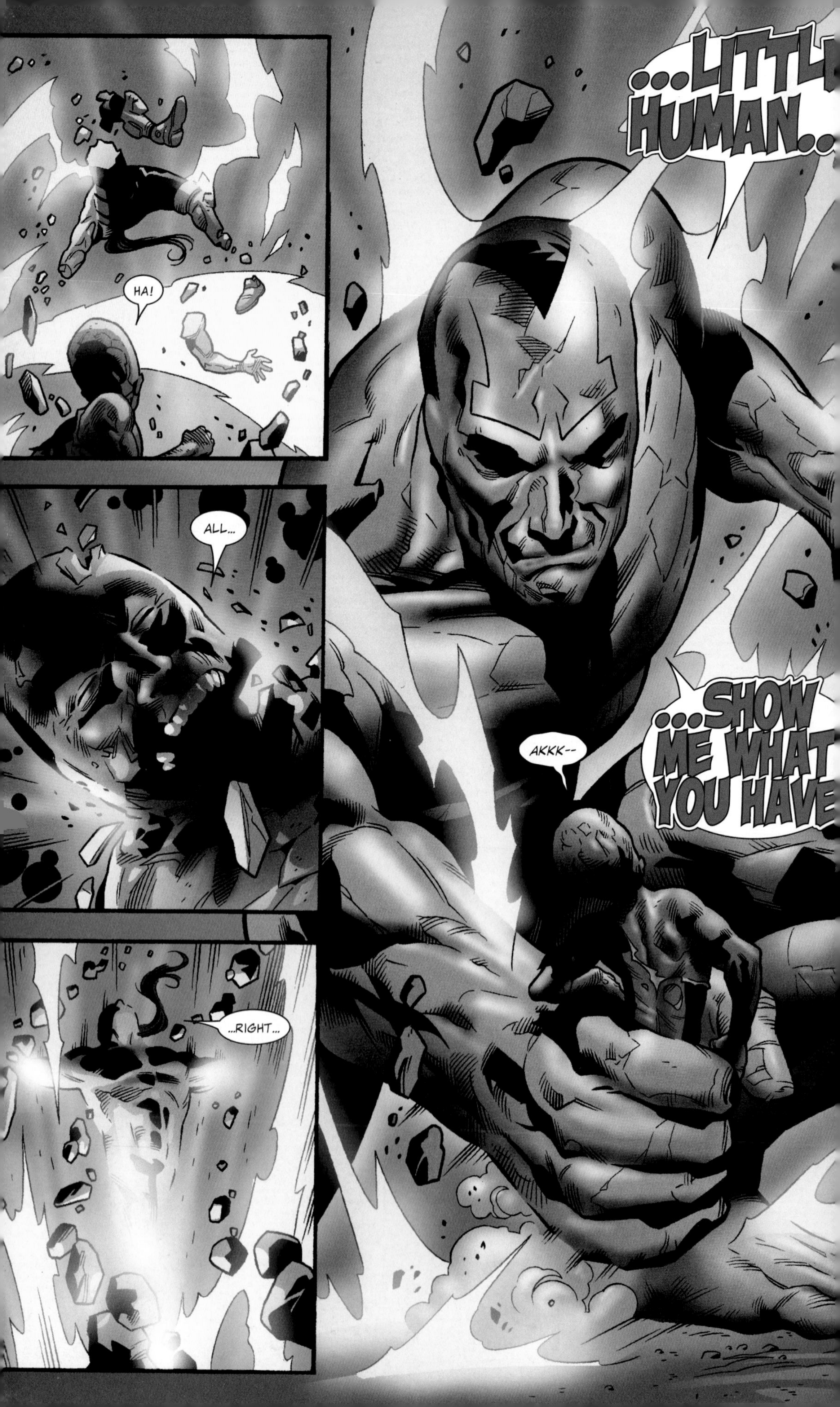
HA!
ALL...
...RIGHT...
...LITTL
HUMAN..
AKKK--
...SHOW
ME WHAT
YOU HAVE

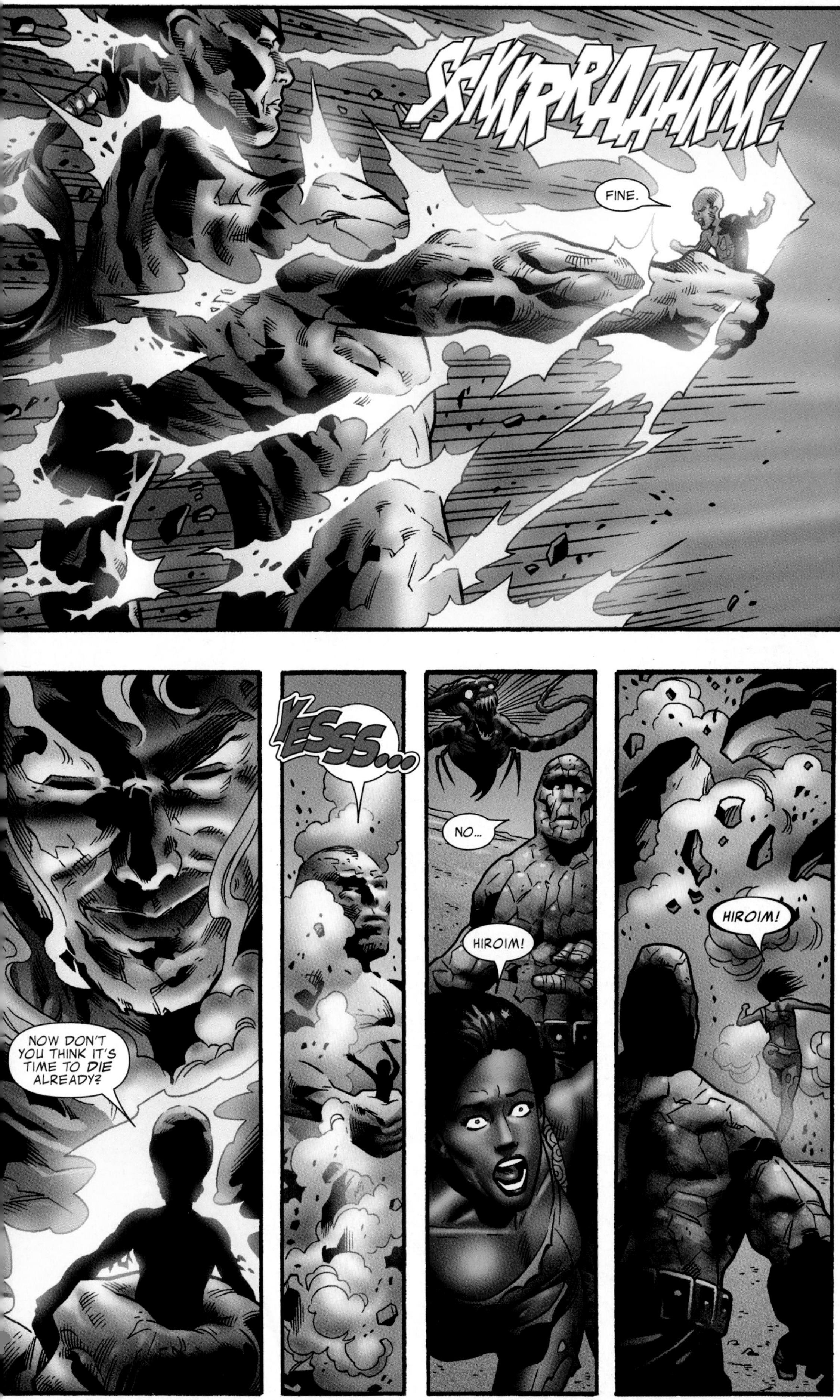
SSKKRRAAAKKK!
FINE.
NOW DON'T YOU THINK IT'S TIME TO DIE ALREADY?
YESSS...
NO...
HIROIM!
HIROIM!

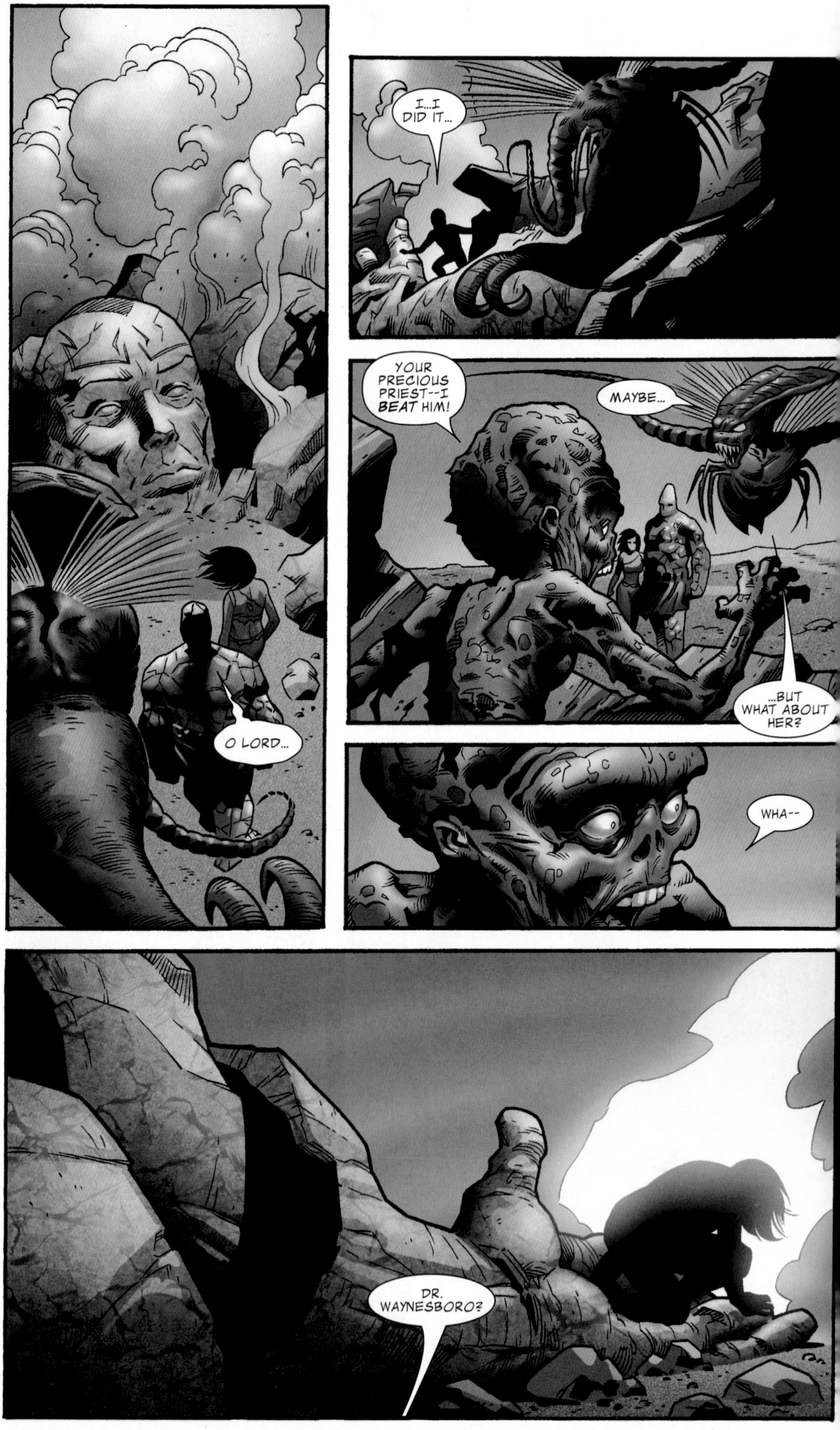

O LORD...
I...I DID IT...
YOUR PRECIOUS PRIEST--I BEAT HIM!
MAYBE...
...BUT WHAT ABOUT HER?
WHA--
DR. WAYNESBORO?

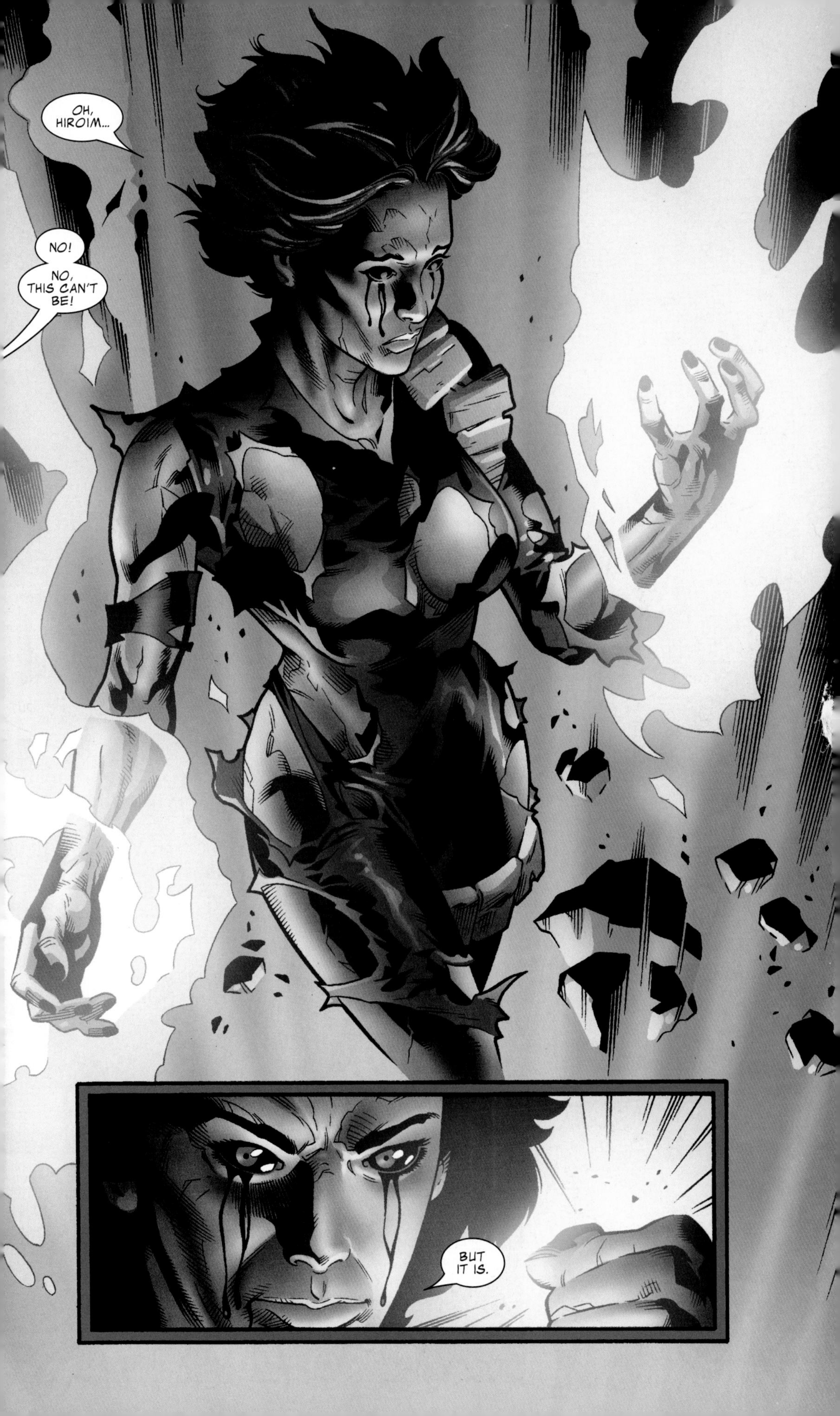
OH, HIROIM...
NO!
NO, THIS CAN'T BE!
BUT IT IS.

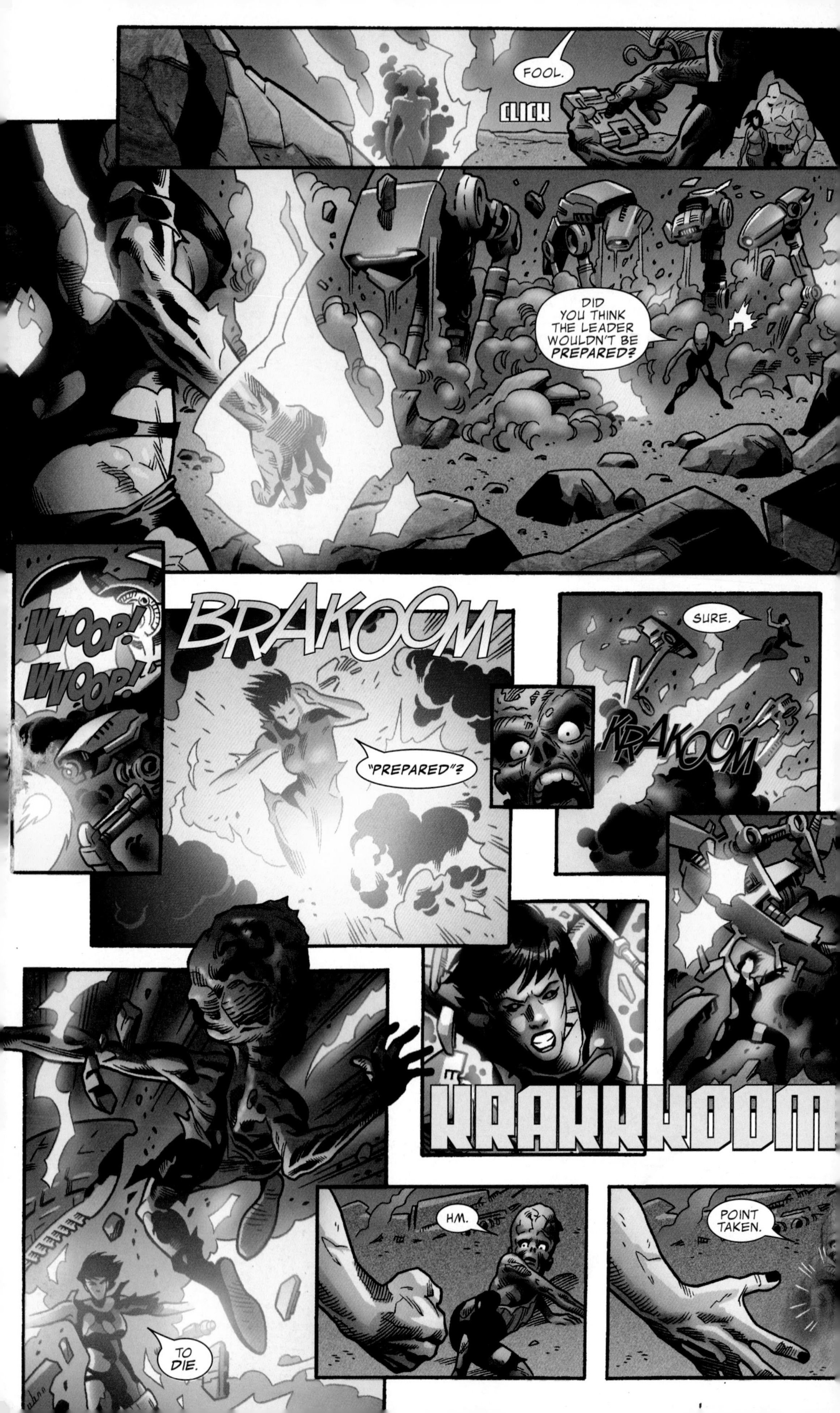
FOOL.
CLICK
DID YOU THINK THE LEADER WOULDN'T BE PREPARED?
WVOOP! WVOOP!
BRAKOOM
"PREPARED"?
SURE.
KRAKOOM
KRAKKKOOM
TO DIE.
HM.
POINT TAKEN.

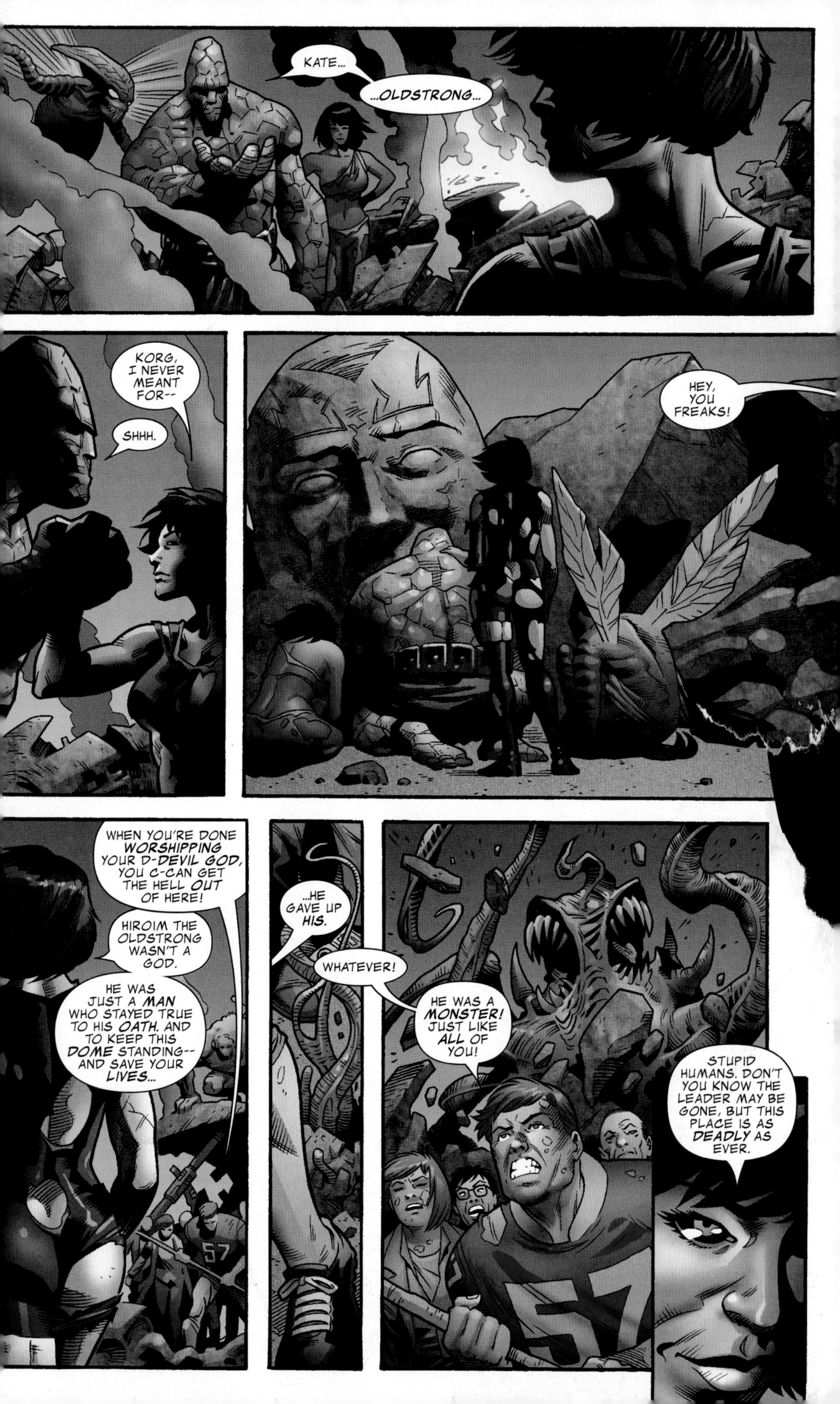
KATE...
...OLDSTRONG...
KORG, I NEVER MEANT FOR--
SHHH.
HEY, YOU FREAKS!
WHEN YOU'RE DONE WORSHIPPING YOUR D-DEVIL GOD, YOU C-CAN GET THE HELL OUT OF HERE!
HIROIM THE OLDSTRONG WASN'T A GOD.
HE WAS JUST A MAN WHO STAYED TRUE TO HIS OATH. AND TO KEEP THIS DOME STANDING-- AND SAVE YOUR LIVES...
...HE GAVE UP HIS.
WHATEVER!
HE WAS A MONSTER! JUST LIKE ALL OF YOU!
STUPID HUMANS. DON'T YOU KNOW THE LEADER MAY BE GONE, BUT THIS PLACE IS AS DEADLY AS EVER.

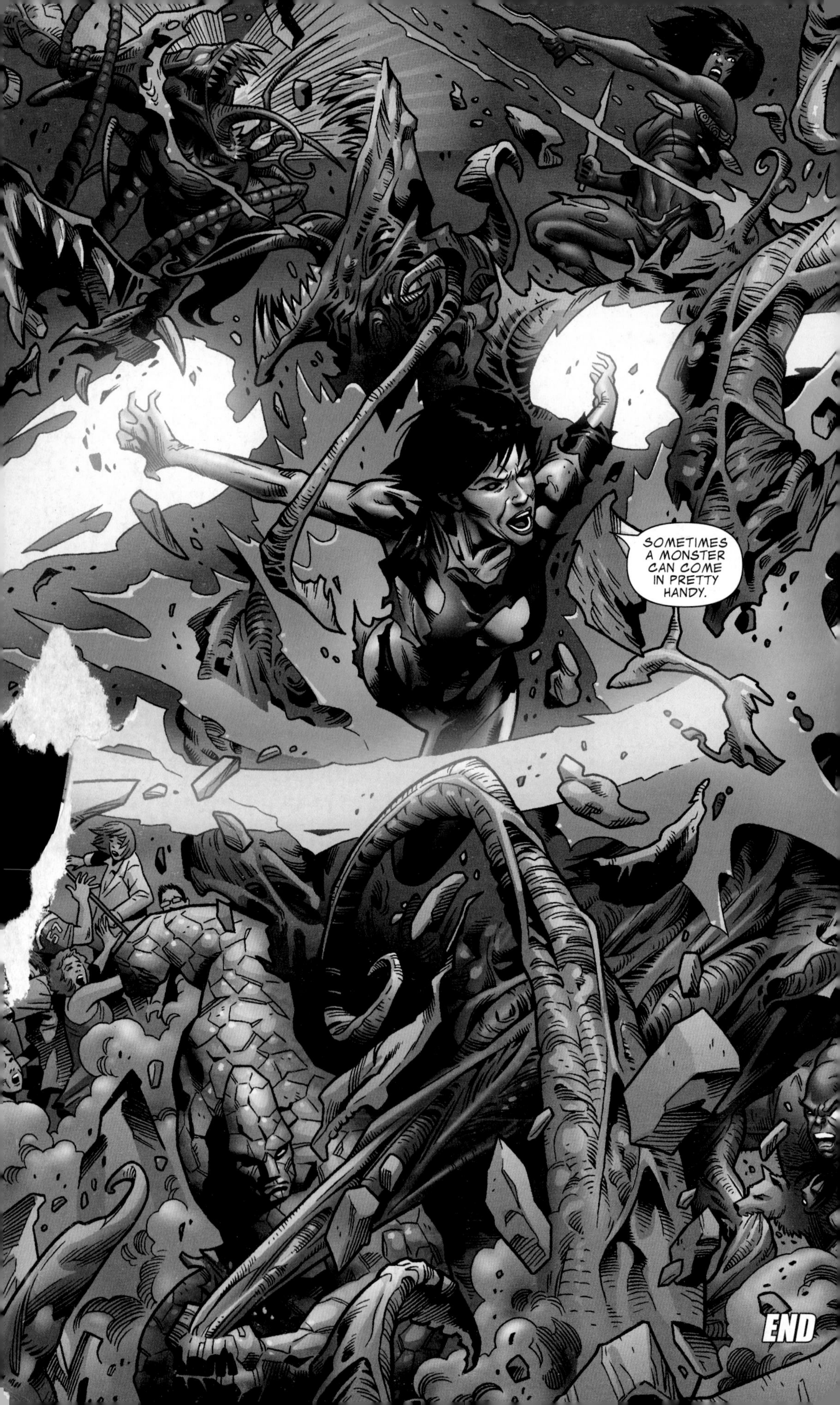
SOMETIMES A MONSTER CAN COME IN PRETTY HANDY.
END